Albanian Social and Philosophical Thinking of the '30s—
Neo–Albanianism

Also by

Irena Nikaj, PhD

Associate Professor

2012 Sociology-3rd ed., albPAPER, Tirana, Albania.

2011 Albanian Social and Philosophical Thinking of the '30s-Neo-Albanianism, 2 end ed., albPAPER, Tirana, Albania.

2006 Sociology of Education, Kotti, Korça, Albania

2004 Sociology-2end ed. Kotti, Korça, Albania

2002 Albanian Social and Philosophical Thinking of the '30s-Neo-Albanianism, Kotti, Korça, Albania

2001 Sociology-1st ed., Afërdita, Tirana, Albania

The published Lectures

2003 Psychology

2003 History of Arts and Cultural Heritage

2003 Sociology of Education

1995 Sociology

E-mail address:inikaj@yahoo.com
@RENANIKAJ

Albanian Social and Philosophical Thinking of the '30s—

Neo-Albanianism

Monograph

Irena Nikaj

English language Consultant

Nicole Centgraf

Florenc Mene

Scientific Editor

Prof. Dr Zyhdi Dervishi

3

AuthorHouse™ LLC
1663 Liberty Drive
Bloomington, IN 47403
www.authorhouse.com
Phone: 1-800-839-8640

Published by AuthorHouse   12/20/2013

ISBN: 978-1-4772-8182-6 (sc)
ISBN: 978-1-4772-8183-3 (hc)
ISBN: 978-1-4772-8184-0 (e)

Library of Congress Control Number: 2012919701

To my parents

He thought of the peoples who lived on the left side of the Empire and of those who lived on the right; of those who had many dreams and those who had few; of those who were quite ready to tell their dreams and those, like Albanians, who were very reserved about them...

The Palace of Dreams by Ismail Kadare

Table of Contents

Foreword by Prof. Dr Zyhdi DERVISHI

An excellent Book of contemporary Values

The first version of this book complied with the standards of a doctoral dissertation defended at the Philosophy-Sociology Department in the University of Tirana. It was written in the 1996-1997 time period, in the most troubled years (even to the point of bloodshed) of the most troubled period of the post-communist transition of Albanian society. While many writers, artists and researchers all but suspended their creative activities under the psychological pressure of political and psycho-spiritual disorder, Irena Nikaj kept on working with persistence and high intensity in order to produce a book titled "Albanian Social and Philosophical Thinking of the '30s (Neo-Albanianism)". Despite the current of events in Albanian society, from the beginning of the '90s (of the previous century) until today, Irena Nikaj has worked incessantly in the area of sociological research, thus constantly increasing the quantity and quality of sociological scientific publications. To this very day, Irena Nikaj is the most conspicuous among female sociologists in the Republic of Albania; she has published more original scientific literature in the area of sociological research than any other professor of sociological subjects who works at a university within the Albanian territory.

In the '30s of the twentieth century, through the pages of more than 300 journals and newspapers, the most notable Albanian thinkers, especially the most well-educated writers, journalists and clergy, wrote and debated widely on the most complicated and most important economic, political, social, and psycho-cultural issues of current and future emancipation and development in Albanian society. In this intellectual enterprise, which was sensitive as well as difficult, the Neo-Albanians school of thought took shape. Its main representatives were e Vangjel Koça, and so on. The thinkers of this line of thought, through vigorous polemics with representatives of other schools of thought, were able to create the clearest, best argued, and most illuminated vision regarding the development of Albanian society. Along the same lines, this book written by Irena Nikaj, a professor of sociological subjects, represents the most complete, well-argued and qualitative scientific research work related to the achievements of the social and philosophical thought of Neo-Albanianism.

This monograph constitutes an invaluable contribution to Albanian sociological studies, at least in the following main aspects:

Firstly, the author has professionally "scanned" the entire literature published by representatives of Neo-Albanianism as well as the literature that published the counter-arguments posed by representatives of other schools of thought that did not agree with neo-Albanians. Through this kind of scanning, the original value of the thoughts developed by neo-Albanian thinkers has been clearly delineated. Among others, the neo-Albanian school of thought argued for the indispensability of cultivating a critical and non-conformist spirit among Albanians. This kind of spirit would help Albanians overcome traditional conservative phenomena and adopt modern patterns of thinking and behavior. The Neo-Albanianism representatives, as Irena Nikaj emphasizes, "... being deeply knowledgeable of a number of philosophical systems and realizing the need of a broader communication of Albanian thinking with Europe's intellectual developments..., appreciate the non-conformism displayed by positivism...", as a mental instrument for the rapid change and multifaceted progress of Albanian society(p. 27).

The argumentation processes of Neo-Albanianism representatives and the generalizations that were professionally achieved on the part of researcher Irena Nikaj sound very relevant for our time. Albanian society is in great need of revivifying its non-conformist spirit as a "mechanism" that helps in finding the most rational solutions to the most complicated issues as well as in diagnosing and overcoming the cankerous wounds of corruption, which is corroding the contemporary Albanian society.

Secondly, according to the perspective of Neo-Albanianism representatives, the new Albanian society (i.e., the modernized Albanian society) would only be constructed by illuminated people, that is, by people of thinking and action. In this way, Albanian society would overcome sluggishness and would be involved in a more vigorous dynamic of multifaceted developments, which would imitate the standards of the most urbanized Western countries. This kind of argumentation, clearly developed by Neo-Albanianism representatives and excellently delineated in the pages of this monograph, stands in contrast to two quite problematic tendencies in contemporary Albanian society:

- The increasing number of those Albanians who spend much time in vacuous theoretical discussions but do not get practically engaged in solving diverse issues; and

- The increasing number of those people who neglect mastering theoretical knowledge and, because they base their thinking only on empirical experience, do not show a correct approach to solving issues.

Thirdly, Irena Nikaj analyzes the "magma" of ideas cultivated by Neo-Albanianism representatives before the '70s and '80s according to a perspective that tries to update its thinking to the framework of relevant and current developments in Albanian society. It is especially for this reason that the monograph titled "Albanian Social and Philosophical Thinking of the '30s—Neo-Albanianism" has not only theoretical, but also, practical value in the treatment and solution of the many complicated issues that are plaguing Albanian society at present. By introducing an excellent and quite visionary theoretical analysis, this book will preserve its theoretical and practical value even in the future.

Introduction

This monograph analyzes a specific part of Albanian social and philosophical thinking in the years '30 of the twentieth century, namely, Neo-Albanianism.

The reasons for this analysis are treated here below.

In post-1990 writings of a research nature, I have encountered many assessments that evaluate the pluralism of thought that emanated from the studies and publications of the '30s, and I have seen the endeavors made by representatives of Albanian thinking to find ways of integrating Albania into Europe. In general, they were of the opinion that this integration could be achieved through progress in the area of governance, as well as through faster developments in the economic, educational, cultural, philosophical realms, and so on.

If we evaluate this period and its values from the present vantage point of intellectual achievements in Europe, perhaps it would not strike us as very illustrious. But, if we bear in mind the history of Albania during the second half of the 20th century—with all those dim chiaroscuro created by the communist dictatorship as well as with the suppression of free thinking— then, we will surely become aware that the Albania of the 1930s lacked numerous things. For this reason, it needed a boost on its road to development, and its advance needed more work and creative energies on the part of Albanians in general, and the people of thinking in particular.

Among other things, the pluralistic character was the main feature of Albanian thinking in the 1930s. As such, it dealt with diverse, and even contradictory, viewpoints and theories. These conceptions were presented through theoretical debates, generally of a liberal and democratic orientation. The overarching subject in such debates was finding the most appropriate methods for Albania's development and its integration into the main current of European development.

Thus, the study of these viewpoints would have not only historical values but also, to a certain extent, actual practical value, because some objectives and developments in Albanian society during the last ten years bear a certain affinity to those of the 1930s. Furthermore, after the Second World War, for a long spell, the worth of the thinking of 1930s was denied: the cultivators of the thought of this period were enshrouded by silence, some of them being forced either to annihilate their thoughts about the liberal and democratic development of Albania or, even worse, flee their motherland.

Leafing through the press and the periodicals of the time, I have had the opportunity to become acquainted with a mosaic of viewpoints, such as those of the so-called illustrious dictatorship, legalistic worldview, and so forth. Among them, the viewpoints of Neo-Albanians emerge and take a very interesting position. In this period, one may find specific studies of a historical nature, such as, for example: the studies by V. Koka, M. Gelegu, I. Fishta, and I. Goga. The literature of the 1930s also consists of works written during those years, such as those by F. S. Noli, Migjeni, L. Poradeci, H. Stermilli, N. Bulka, as well as studies and monographic works by K. Dako, K. Floqi, Timo Dilo, etc.

In the introduction to his study, "Currents of Sociopolitical Thought in Albania in the '30s of the 20th century", V. Koka opens the door to further studies in this field. Among other things, he writes: Dealing primarily with sociopolitical ideas, which constitute the object of this thesis, we have naturally left outside the scope of this study other issues related to ideology. These may be treated in other special studies.[1]

An understanding of ideology in this study is related to the concept treated by the French philosopher, A. Destutt De Tracy. De Tracy was the first to coin the phrase "the science of ideas", which aspires to discover in man the genesis of his tendencies and judgments.[2] Since the beginning of the 19th century, this

---

1 V. Koka, Currents of Sociopolitical Thought in Albania in the 30 years of XX century, Tirana 1985, pp.9-10.

2 Ideology: the whole of beliefs of a society or a social class (Larousse: Dictionary of Philosophy, SHBE, Tiranë 1994; A word coined by the French philosopher Destutt de Tracy (Élements d'idéologie, 1801-5) to denote the "science o ideas"(The Fontana Dictionary of Modern Thought, Edit. A. Bullock & O. Stallybrass, 1977); the word was revived with the publication in 1927 of Marx's previosly unpublished

concept-phrase has been used primarily to characterize the ideals, convictions, values and viewpoints of the world's, religious beliefs, political philosophies, and moral reasoning.

L. Dumont, on the other hand, pushes this concept even further in an endeavor to bridge the academic divide between social anthropology and ideology (or the history of ideas, to use his own phrase). His opinion is that his work, "Essays on Individualism", may cross the academic distinction that divides the specialty of "social science," viz., social anthropology; from a study that treats "the history of ideas," or the intellectual history of our modern western civilization. In other words, he tries to show how a study of the characteristic entirety of ideas and values of modernity is legitimate and even appropriate... And this is not difficult because, to begin with, inspiration for this study has a face and name. His name is Marcel Mauss (Dumont, L., 1997: 9).

Proceeding along the path blazed by all the previous studies, my treatise aims at continuing to give the dimensions of Albanian thinking in the 1930s, and my focus will center on the social, philosophical, aesthetic, sociological, and psychological thought of Neo-Albanianism. It is my opinion that despite its deficiencies Neo-Albanianism tried, more than all others, to make present among Albanians Europe's (past and contemporary) philosophical and scientific viewpoints. In so doing, Neo-Albanianism created the first beginnings of an independent reasoning, with the noble aim of creating an Albanian social and philosophical thought according to the most progressive western paradigms.

The viewpoints of the main representatives of Neo-Albanianism, which constitute the object of this study, are to be found dispersed in diverse periodicals of the contemporary press and

---

The German Ideology, and in 1929 (translated 1936) of K. Manheim's "Ideology and Utopia", as J. Plamenatz puts it, a "family of Concepts".—Lionel Trilling in The Liberal Imagination, 1950, defined it as "the habit or the ritual of showing respect for certain formulas to which, for various reasons having to do with emotional safety, we have very strong ties of whose meaning and consequences in actuality we have no clear understanding"; see also Larousse: Dictionary of Philosophy, p.166.

constitute a time extension from December 1928 – when Neo-Albanian thinking was foreseen by Gjirokastra's "Demokratia" newspaper – until the January-March 1939 edition of "The Albanian Endeavor". In the December 1928 edition of "Demokratia", Branko Merxhani writes that "the issue of Neo-Albanianism is an issue of creation. Every element it possesses is waiting the hour of its creation: past, present, and future!" However, in one of the final issues of the "Albanian Endeavor", this same author writes: "... until we are able to write history, we must, first of all, do a lot of preparatory work of great importance. We have a task that will take at least another half a century. Until then, let us leave the glory of writing history to the mania and pleasure of those who are able to fill entire pages and volumes by simply dipping their mediocre pen in a black ink bottle, or in ink mixed with a few drops of... water!"[3]

I will construct the analysis of their viewpoints based on the classical conception of philosophy and its constituent parts: viz., the issues of knowledge, metaphysics, ethics, science, history, religions, arts, and morality. The main sources for achieving my purpose were the theoretic articles published in the press of the 1930s and, first and foremost, in the "Albanian Endeavor" and "Illyria" periodicals. Nonetheless, other publications were also analyzed, which have helped create a more complete knowledge regarding this issue. Furthermore, I also studied other works of a documentary, artistic, and cultural nature that were published in the 1930s, as well as studies published later.

Other resources used were a number of works and opinions of diverse thinkers and philosophers, from Greek philosophy down to other thinkers who, in my opinion, constitute the Pleiades of thinking and reason on the relation, or relations, that they have to the issue we are studying.

In the end of introduction I owe a great debt and I want to thank the following people in particular for the diverse forms of help they given me: Prof. Dr Zyhdi Dervishi, my mentor; Prof. Dr

---

3B. Merxhani, "History and Historiography", Magazine "Albanian Endeavor", No.18-24, Tirana 1938, p.240.

Artan Fuga, Mimoza Zografi–Shpata, PhD and Petrika Shpata, Prof. asc. Dr Aleksandra Piluri.

Thank you!

II. The historical place of New Albanianism

There is no question that Neo-Albanianism takes a conspicuous position in the intellectual challenge of the '30s in the 20th century. This part of the social, philosophical, aesthetic, artistic (etc.) thought was developed through polemics with the viewpoints of other currents, especially that of the "illustrious dictatorship", the legalists, the communistic viewpoints, and so forth.

In a more generalizing characterization, Neo-Albanianism represents an entirety of viewpoints of a democratic nature, which tend toward the prioritized evaluation of the illuminating role of knowledge, science, and culture.

The National Profile of the Neo-Albanian Trend

As a trend, Neo-Albanianism demonstrates, *first of all*, elements of a national nature that can be evaluated, and constitutes, in my opinion, the most refined and most complete national viewpoint. Focusing on this aspect, we may say that Neo-Albanianism may be defined as new nationalism, or the nationalism of the 1930s. This conclusion may be attained based on the relations that Neo-Albanianism creates with the past of the Albanian people– a past that is historical, economic, political, cultural, and intellectual.

According to the views of the main representatives of this trend, the periods when Albanian patriotism created its fundamental elements were the age of Skanderbeg and that of the Albanian National Renaissance. While this nationalism was in its infancy during Skanderbeg's time, the National Renaissance period brought more complete components, as well as its completeness. This, in its turn, determined a reasonable and quite positive preface to Albania's future – the declaration of Independence on

28 November 1912 by Ismail Qemali. To support this idea, this trend's main representatives bring forward the argument of the existence of the national ideal during the National Renaissance. In general, the need for the reemergence of such an ideal as the one that appeared during the National Renaissance was considered by them necessary, useful, and indispensable for the Albania of the 1930s.[4]

National Morality – A Synthesis of Values and Norms

Treating the issues of moral as part of philosophical thinking, Neo-Albanianism proponents usually started from the general notion that it is not ideas alone which influence the destiny of a given society, but also its era, as well as the new state of objects, the new conditions of life and its necessities. These, too, exercise a mysterious influence on our ideas and dispositions.[5]

From here, there is a movement from the general sense to the reasoning that all those elements influence a nation's cohesion, where morality holds a special place, according to B. Merxhani: The ideal society was the one that had a lot of spirit and density and, also, the ideal nation was the one that spoke one language, had one morality and used the same kind of tools.[6]

The conception of morality emerges from the notion that, *first of all*, there has been a collective order that has achieved the immediate functioning of the institution in society and, *secondly*, this impacted the societal conscience, bringing as a result the achievement of collective action. The notion of this cohesion and its continuity would have positive values, because it would neutralize the elements that disturbed this cohesion and, primarily, the influences as a result of the coexistence of diverse cultures and values, as well as the continual relations that

---

4V. Nirvana, The Intellectual Year 1936, Magazine "Albanian Endeavor", No.4-5-6, March 1937, p.204.

5Magazine "Illyria", 01. 07. 1934, p. 2.

6Ibid. , 02. 11. 1935, p. 5.

Albanian historically had had with them. In fact, this was so important that only culture and morality created those relations that achieved the nation's existence.[7]

The influence of their beliefs is viewed as a very important action in the moral realm, in the creation of the national morality and education. These were achievable by making a synthesis of the national moral values and norms, but also by deeply appreciating the positive elements of morality and education in their historical development, because this development and these values had created that modern view of morality. Furthermore, the thoughts of R. Descartes, J. Dewey, W. James, and S. Freud are also treated in connection with the moral reflections of their views, as well as for the relations of morality to education. When we speak about education, we see its links to ethics through the concepts of culture and social behavior, elements which tend to review the role of tradition in culture, but also in the realm of morality.

Characteristics of the Ethical Thinking by Neo-Albanians

From this perspective, the main proponents of Neo-Albanianism expressed their position on the theoretical evaluation of ethics, as well as on the evaluation of the moral traditions that characterize the ethno-psychological nature of Albanians.

B. Merxhani treats the ethical thought communicated by R. Descartes as a thought that was not openly revealed. This was related not only to the direct impact of his philosophy on the human moral stance, but also to the fact that his philosophy was not viewed favorably and was not approved by the morality of the time, when religion was still exercising strong control on the human moral stance and on the honoring of moral norms that stemmed from the dogma of accepting God as the supreme value.

7Magazine "Albanian Endeavor", No. 4-5-6, March 1937, p. 222.

Here is how B. Merxhani expresses his thoughts on R. Descartes and his moral views: Descartes has always articulated his moral thoughts in such formulas, articulated with prudence and never openly. We may say that our Philosopher, in his descriptions of moral principles, used the same writing tactics that Persia's philosopher-poet, Omar Khayyam, used centuries before him[*] in relation to the fanatics of his own day, trying always to put the mantel of poetic symbolism on his new ideas. This Philosopher's sorrows, which came from the restrictions of the time that never allowed him the freedom to demonstrate his ideas, are also indirectly expressed in his phrase that … such ado was made on my poor physical principles that I don't know what they would have done had I dealt with Morality![8]

What is, according to Neo-Albanians, the indirect view given by R. Descartes on morality and moral values?

B. Merxhani examines the thought pronounced by J. G. Mayer concerning the fundamentals of the Cartesian method and, according to the latter, the axis of this method (R. Descartes's – I. N.) is the criterion of rational evidence. Also, according to J. G. Mayer (cited by the most illustrious representative of Neo-Albanianism), this stance toward inherited truths inaugurates[*] the "*critical philosophy*", which would be continued by E. Kant. This is exactly the point where R. Descartes cuts his ties to the past, the moldy traditions, the untouchable authority, and the prejudices collected and blindly advocated by philosophers until then.[9]

Further on, J. G. Mayer reveals a classical aspect of Cartesianism from a practical perspective. It is demonstrated, not in the

---

[*]It comes to persian polymath: philosopher, mathematician, astronomer and poet Omar Khayyàm, author of "Rubayiat"-I. N.

[8]B. Merxhani, The moral Philosophy of Descartes, Magazine "Albanian Endeavor", No. 9-10, p. 177.

[*] appears for the first time-I.N.

[9]J. G. Mayer, Philosophical and moral Values of Cartesianism, Magazine "Albanian Endeavor", No. 9-10, August 1937, p. 163.

absolute respect for the established authority, but in the hierarchy principle. After a coordination of thoughts, there should also be subordination between people, because these are different by nature – says J. G. Mayer.[10]

R. Descartes himself thinks that the practical value of norms may be illustrated by the example of some travelers who have lost their bearings and, instead of going around in circles; they walk always in one direction. In the same way, when we cannot recognize which thoughts are right, we should follow those that are more likely to respond to our goal. This is due to the fact that the human spirit possesses something divine, where the seeds of useful thoughts have been planted since its inception and, no matter how frequently our efforts thwarted, we nevertheless, bear unexpected fruits.[11]

According to B. Merxhani, R. Descartes considers philosophy the root of the scientific tree, while morality is the flower of this tree.[12] Defining R. Descartes' morality as a provisory morality and discovering its links to Stoical morality, B. Merxhani aims at laying out morality's stable elements that appear as tradition, alongside the changes that occur and that are connected to the tree (namely, philosophy) and to the changes that occur in society that condition change in moral values and norms. From within these changes, the link between morality and education appears. Dh. Shuteriqi also gives an evaluation of this issue by comparing the pragmatist views with the functionalist views.

S. Treska also treats issue in the spirit of pragmatism, while other authors, such as V. Koça, L. Skëndo, and A. Xhuvani, tend more toward the treatment of values in a direct relationship with the needs of the country's development and the qualitative progress in this area as well.

Relying on the functionalist views of E. Durkheim, Dh. Shuteriqi writes: We should know that, in order to appreciate the existence

---

10J. G. Mayer, Philosophical and moral Values of Cartesianism, Magazine "Albanian Endeavor", No. 9-10, August 1937, p. 165.

11Ibid., p. 168.

12Ibid., p. 164.

of society, education should provide the citizens with an adequate unity of ideas and feelings, without which society would be impossible; and in order that it may yield this result, it should not be left entirely into the hands of specific people.[13] Further on, Dh. Shuteriqi, evaluating what the school should achieve in the moral realm, emphasizes social power and social interest. Basing his reasoning on pragmatist views, he shows the sources that pragmatism has relied on in order to work out its own views.

According to him, J. S. Mill and E. Kant are those who have best defined the essence of education, which aims at developing within each individual all the perfection that he/she is able to acquire. Whatever the importance of specific educations, each of them are based on one common foundation: there are no people without a number of ideas, feelings, and practices–says Dh. Shuteriqi. Education must not fail to instill in all of their children, whatever their social status. Because every society has formed some kind of human ideal in the intellectual, physical and moral sense, this ideal is, to a certain extent, common to all its members. Furthermore, morality is closely related to the nature of societies; it changes when these change; hence, it is the product of communal living. The idea and sense of order and discipline (outwardly as well as inwardly) have been etched in our consciences by society.[14]

According to Dh. Shuteriqi, moral values are related to the society's level of development, as well as to the condition of the society's institutional organization. While the development of these institutions is closely linked to its form of governance, whatever form the governance may assume has great impact on the observation of moral norms by the individuals. This, according to him, is related to the authority and freedom between these two elements that are present in the process of the individual's education and progress. To him, authority and freedom are not two words that stand in contradistinction to each other, but are closely related. Freedom, writes Dh. Shuteriqi, is

13Magazine "Albanian Endeavor", No. 4-5-6, Tirana, March 1937, p. 222.

14Magazine "Albanian Endeavor", No.17, Tirana, May 1938, f. 280.

the daughter of authority, when it is well-understood. However, being free does not mean doing whatever you like, but being master of yourself, knowing how to act on judgments and fulfilling your duty. [15]

Starting from this understanding, we must emphasize that the author is trying to interpret moral norms as imperative norms, which are not *a priori* norms, and here he departs from the naturalist ethical understanding of norms and tends towards an intertwined understanding of the common norms with their consequences. Further, this is included in the axiological sense, also taking a relative nature, which means that, norms, as well as moral values, have their relativity. In our opinion, this is related to the judgment of the individual and his action, or to the judgments he gives on things outside him, evaluating them from within the moral theory or axiological system as observations or evaluations of specific situations and states.

In his reasoning on morality, S. Treska tends to rely not only on E. Kant's views, but also on those of H. Spencer and the pragmatists; thus, his views also rely on empiricism, which is characteristic of pragmatist. S. Treska also evaluates the moral reflexes of the psychological elements, using as an argument treatises in the realm of individual psychology conducted by A. Adler.

S. Treska notes that even though man is a being with moral principles and education, he is influenced by biological—H. Spencer, however, S. Treska appreciates E. Kant's view that education, viewed as the entirety of man's moral principles and values, has the capability of deeply influencing man; in fact, according to E. Kant, man may become man only by means of education–he is only what education makes him to be. [16]

Reasoning in a pragmatist manner, he emphasizes that a moral principle is right when it leads us into useful directions. [17] S.

15Ibid., p. 282.

16S. Treska, Biology and Education, Magazine "Albanian Endeavour", No 13, Tirana, January 1938, pp.13-15.

17Ibid., p. 18.

Treska mentions the role of morality and its values in the practical realm, because, from a pragmatist viewpoint, the only education that is of value and may be properly called "education"–in the sense of morality– is only that education which is rooted in daily life and in the things with which man deals on a daily basis.[18]

V. Koça links morality to ideas and ideals, treating them as spiritual values that influence human activity through the path they choose, the actions they take and the judgments they make on them. V. Koça deems ethics as an element that strengthens national consciousness. In fact, he deems moral tradition as extremely important for Albania, because it is a factor that helps preserve the spiritual and national continuity of nation.[19] Further, moral traditions are a support for evading the danger of Communism. He thinks that it is the heroic spirit of the past that will bring spiritual freedom.[20]

L. Skëndo's views, within the line of relations between moral values and national consciousness, say that tradition has a huge influence; to put it simply, the past is very important since it constitutes a nation's history. According to him, the study of history is ought to be respected just as the sanctity of religious beliefs is respected; it has strongly influenced – and continues to influence – our feelings and emotions. Moreover, he goes on to say that the present, the past and, most importantly, the future of a people depends on its feelings and ideas.[21]

In A. Xhuvani's opinion, moral values are deemed necessary for the formation of man's personality and for his good behaviors. Analyzing his arguments concerning this issue in their entirety, we think that A. Xhuvani is under the influence of the moral

---

18Ibid., No. 11-12, Tirana, September 1937, p. 213.

19Ibid., p. 7.

20Ibid., p. 7.

21Magazine "Albanian Endeavor", No. 4-5-6, Tirana, March 1937, p. 231.

theory on personality and the psycho-moral elements as its constituent elements.[22]

B. Merxhani links the need for morality with the ideal and here, he approaches V. Koça's stance. However, V. Koça's position does not consider ethics as part of philosophy. In order to give a general evaluation, B. Merxhani quotes F. Nietzsche, who argues that every people, if it wants to live on and to prove itself, should; first of all, organize chaos into its Ego.[23] Ideal turns man from an egotist into an altruist.[24]

Relying on R. Descartes' views, as well as on those of E. Durkheim, B. Merxhani contends that moral values achieve a sort of homogenization within society, a melting together of spirits, of feeling the same.[25] On the other hand, these moral values and norms create relationships and, moreover, strengthen existing relationships, creating social solidarity and thus helping to create an ideal cohesion. In fact, B. Merxhani considers the influence of moral norms as more potent than the impact of the state, because they put human action into motion, and this is inherent in the Albanian tradition. Through moral rules and norms in Albanian society, the relations between people have been regulated for long historical periods.

In the realm of moral values, B. Merxhani does not hesitate to also provide the qualification that not every moral tradition is valuable. Preserving tradition may be as positive as its avoidance in the name of historical development.[26] The power of tradition may be the power of sluggishness, and nations have preformed miracles exactly when they departed from the old traditions and took on new elements.[27] Bearing S. Freud's opinion in mind,

---

22A. Xhuvani, Personality, Magazine "Albanian Endeavor", No. 16, April 1938, pp. 181-184.

23Magazine "Illyria", No. 15, 1934, p. 1.

24Newspaper "Demokratia", 09. 03. 1929, p. 3.

25Magazine "Illyria", 02. 11. 1935, p. 5.

26Newspaper "Demokratia", 29. 07. 1933, p. 3.

27B. Merxhani, Tradition and nationa Idea, Magazine "Illyria", 17. 12. 1935, p. 5.

Merxhani sees value, norm, and moral duty as elements that suppress desire and achieve a moral judgment inspired by high spiritual functions, with which man is equipped. Here, moral consciousness, according to him, is identified with consciousness or conscience.[28] For him, moral values function as a protection against outer danger—namely, against foreign colonization.

Albania–Built by "The People of Thinking" and "The People of Action"

According to the definitions provided by the main proponents of Neo-Albanianism, patriotism is related to the developments of the 1930s and the need for progress in the Albanian society of the period. According to them, these developments were related to the values achieved by Albanians throughout their history, but were also very closely related to the Albanian reality of their time. Consequently, the Neo-Albanian stance toward the Albanian state in the 1930s was a positive one. It can be called positive because, generally speaking, they accept the Albanian state in its political and monarchical form, with King Zog I as its head, and, at the same time, they present arguments for such a stance.

According to Neo-Albanians, with the monarchy created by Zog, almost all the Albanian endeavors for independence– as well as the creation and strengthening of their state– were positively brought to successful fruition.[29] The monarchy ushered in the new period of developing a "strong intellectual, civilizing" activity.[30] Furthermore, according to them, Zog's regime and his administration constituted "the people of action." Neo-Albanians referred to themselves as "people of thinking" and wrote that, by

---

28B. Merxhani, Five lectures on Psycho-Analysis, Magazine "Albanian Endeavor", No. 17, Tirana, May 1938, pp. 283-290.

29Newspaper Demokratia, 08.12.1928, p.1 dhe 01.01.1929.

30Newspaper Demokratia, 07.03.1931, p.5.

cooperating with the "people of action", they would build Albania's future.[31]

B. Merxhani, who was one of the most prominent proponents of Neo-Albanianism, viewed the monarchical regime as a "positive" one, whose objective was to struggle against "anti-social tendencies" and also to attain a process of progress that "would raise the society to the level of culture and civilization."[32]

In addition to the appreciation of the role of the monarchy and the special role they attributed to themselves, the representatives of this trend, in supporting the process of Albania's progress in general, also promoted and defended the governmental cabinets. The governmental cabinets together with the parliament (according to them) were the initiators of the introduction and implementation of the political, cultural and social policies in Albania which set up the framework for the strategy of its capitalistic development. Expressing his opinion on the activity of Mehdi Frasheri's governmental cabinet, B. Merxhani emphasized that he would achieve not only national unity, but also the creation of a society with a "harmonious and sincere atmosphere" on the road toward "the strengthening of contacts between power and the people".[33]

Furthermore, the instrumentalization of democracy was deemed a natural and most important process for the Albanian society, through which, by means of the election process (similar to the election model of western societies, but also with some Albanian specifics), it was hoped to achieve a natural progress in this area.

According to Neo-Albanians, an election model that was similar to that of western countries could be attained in big towns such as "Gjirokastra, Vlora, Korça, Durres, Shkoder, and so forth," whereas, in less developed regions, the election system of secondary electors could still be used.[34]

31Newspaper Demokratia, 22.12.1928, p.2,23.03.1929, f.2.

32Newspaper "People's Will", 28.11.1930, p.3.

33Magazine "Illyria", 26.10.1935, p.1.

34Newspaper "Demokratia" 16.11.1929, p.1.

In their examination of European political experiences and methods of organizing, the proponents of Neo-Albanianism analyzed not only the traditional western bourgeois system, but also the fascist system and the model constructed in Turkey by Mustafa Kemal Ataturk. The fascist regime, in general, was deemed by them as inappropriate for Albania, because, according to B. Merxhani, it was only appropriate for semi-capitalist social systems and structures and inappropriate for the systems and structures in developed countries, as well as for non-capitalist systems and structures such as that of Albania.[35]

Press publications, where the views of Neo-Albanian thinking were echoed–such as "Demokratia", "Illyria", and "Albanian Endeavor", were also the venue for the delineation of their ideas, which aimed at creating an Albanian philosophy, according to the need for the processing of the sociological, psychological, pedagogical and cultural thought. This was viewed as an indispensable advancement in light of the level of development and the further perspectives of such development, as well as in connection to the need for a qualitative increase in Albanian philosophical thinking.

At the time when these views were cultivated–by this, we mean the time period of 1928-1939–Albania was a somewhat consolidated state, which publicly declared its objective to walk on the road of accelerating the economic development of its own country. At the head of the Albanian state– which after 1928 assumed the shape of a monarchy– was Ahmed Zog. According to researcher B. J. Fisher, Zog's government was the marriage of western political doctrines with Eastern despotism. Zog is presented as the true builder of the Albanian state and, what is more, he is also given credit for the transformation of the Albanian state into a western-type state.[36]

---

35 B. Merxhani, "What is the good of Kamalism for us", Magazine "Minerva", Tiranë, July, 1935, p.2.

36 B.J.Fischer, "King Zog and the Struggle for Stability in Albania", Çabej, Tirana, 1996, p.15. Zog I, (Ahmed Bey Zog) (1895-1961), King of the Albanians. Albanian politician who joined the Austrians during the first World War; leiter was prime minister (1922-24), president (1925-28), King (1928-39). In March 1925 a new constitution was approved which invested the president with virtually dictatorial powers On September 1, 1928, Zog realized his ultimate

In the 1930s, Albanian economy experienced a number of developments, especially in the agricultural area. In this context of economic progression, it was natural for Albanian thinkers to search for the possibility of finding ways of qualitative developments in the area of thinking. This was reflected in the pluralism of views that were processed and made known at the time, primarily through diverse press publications and especially in magazines.

Raising the need for economic reforms, Neo-Albanians took into account many experiences in diverse countries with the aim of using them in Albania. To this end, they analyzed Mustafa Kemal Ataturk's experience in the area of economic reforms and the republican system he had set up in Turkey. According to V. Koça, "Kemalism" meant not only progress for Turkey, but it was also more appropriate than fascism for Albanian nature and psychology.[37]

According to the main proponents of this thinking, the *progress-order-rule* formula, viewed from the perspective of Albanian conditions, meant that progress could be advocated and attained

---

ambition-the parliament unanimously proclaimed Albania a hereditary monarchy and Zog assumed the title of "Zog I, King of the Albanians." Zog's royal dictatorship was characterized by a combination of despotism and Western reform. Although Zog continued to practice oppressive policies, his regime enacted a substantial number of reforms. Western-style civil, commercial and penal codes were adopted while some modern facilities and technology were introduced into Albania for the first time. Although Zog succeeded in centralizing his regime's political authority, he was incapable of developing Albania's primitive economy with the domestic resources at his disposal-his policies in this sphere eventually led to his downfall. Zog turned to Italy for assistance During the 1930s Zog attempted on several occasions to lessen Rome's tightening grip on Albania. However, in April 1939, angered by Zog's refusal to transform Albania into an Italian protectorate, Mussolini's forces invaded Albania. The Italian army was met with little resistance, and Zog fled to Greece on April 8, 1939, to join his wife, Geraldine Apponyi of Hungary, whom he had married a year earlier, and his newborn son, Leka. Zog's monarchy came to a formal end on April 12, 1939, when the Albanian parliament abolished the 1928 constitution and proclaimed Albania's union with Rome by offering the crown to the Italian monarch, Victor Emmanuel III (see also Zog I-Encyclopedia of World Biography.2004)

37Newspaper "Demokratia", Gjirokastra, 25.01.1930.

by any regime. Generally speaking, they thought that the road of bourgeois development had already become the principle of progress in Albanian society, and despite its slowness, Albania was already walking on this road.[38] Among other things, B. Merxhani underlines: This development of the society after the bourgeois manner and without turbulences (i.e., without social unrest) suited Albania's bourgeois agricultural structure (small bourgeoisie), which lacked industry and the proletariat. Feudalism was in the process of disintegration and Albania was heading toward democracy as a cultural and economic organization.[39]

In their treatment of the issue of finding ways for Albania's development in agriculture and industry, as well as in the cultural, educational and intellectual areas, Neo-Albanians expounded many views as to the way qualitative progress in agriculture and industry could be achieved by depending on their more general orientations. The main proponents of this thought advocated the idea of agricultural development through state support. They also widely expounded upon the ways to achieve this development. They thought that, in Albania's conditions, the Prussian way was better than the Bolshevik one. ... The Agrarian issue, writes B. Merxhani, should be solved like in the civilized countries, i.e., without turbulences, and without uprisings, but through the gradual dissemination and systematic application of reformatory plans.[40]

Furthermore, they deemed it indispensable to make use of the interest shown by European researchers who completed some studies on Albania's agricultural economic issues.[+] According to

---

38Magazine "Albanian Endeavor", No.3, December 1936, p.176.

39Ibid., pp.176-177.

40Newspapers "Demokratia" 22.12.1928, p.2.

+ [+] New Albanians list: Nowack, Reiseberichte aus Albanien, 1920-23; A. Calmé, La Situation Economique d'Albanie, Geneve, 1922; Louis, (Albanien 1927); Markgraf, Pflanzegeographie von Albanien, 1932; Gross, Wirtschaftsstruktur Albaniens, 1932; Bush-Zantnerit; Agrarreform und Agrarverfasung in Albanien, 1935; G. Lorenzoni, La questione Agraria albanese, Bari 1931; Dr. M.Urban, Die Siedlungen Sudalbaniens, Oehringen 1938.

Neo-Albanians, another very important source alongside the above was Dr D. Zavalani's study titled "Die landwirtschaftlichen Verhältnisse Albaniens", Berlin, Paul Parey 1938. This study by Dr D. Zavalani–an agronomy graduate– makes an analysis of the Albania's agricultural past, on the basis of some statistics constructed by the researcher himself as well as on official statistics, and draws some conclusions on how to develop Albanian agriculture, in which the most reasonable path is concluded to be its capitalist development.[41]

Z. Bejleri treats the issue of agricultural development in relation to the state and the support it has given, and should continue to give, to agriculture. He writes: The Albanian state has done a lot for the farmer, despite the limited means in its disposal. Specifically, the state has helped the farmer with seeds, plows, trees and saplings, and it has also implemented the Agrarian Reform, which gave villagers land at the price of one golden napoleon coin per hectare.[42] This author advocates the notion that agriculture is developed through state support according to the models of some developed European states.

Here, the issue of agrarian credit is also treated, but this is viewed as difficult to achieve. Alongside it, it is deemed that such forms of organization as cooperatives and agricultural unions are also acceptable. Z. Bejleri is of the opinion that banks should support these organizations by allocating personal grants to farmers, just like in the case of Greece and Bulgaria. On the other hand, the in-existence of a Bureau of Land Management was viewed as obstructive; hence, the need for its organization was deemed important.[43]

In general, the proponents of this thinking advocated that economic development was also influenced, to a certain extent,

---

41B. Merxhani, Book review of Dr. D. Zavalanit "Die landëirtschaftlichen Verhältnisse Albaniens", Magazine "Albanian Endeavor", No. 7, May 1930, p.300.

42 Z. Bejleri, Agrucultural Credit, Magazine "Albanian Endeavor", No. 11-12, September 1937, pp.223-228.

43 Ibid., p. 228.

by a country's demographic situation. In relation to the analysis of the country's demographic condition, the studies done by T. Zavalani stand out as prominent. The "Albanian Endeavor" magazine has published some research articles of this nature. Some data that presents interest were those that gave the general number of the Albanian population in 1930–as 1,003,097 inhabitants, the population density by prefectures.

Tirana	Durrësi	Berat	Korça	Vlora	Gjirokastra	Elbasan	Dibra	Shkodra	Kosova
67	52	42	41	40	35	30	30	21	21

Table1. The population density by prefectures

According to T. Zavalani, economic development is not hugely related to population density. This conclusion is primarily based on the comparative analysis of the population density in Korça and Vlora, which, in terms of general development, had no apparent distinction from Tirana and Durres.[44] On the other hand, based on statistics during 1931-1938, he comes to the conclusion that the demographic tendency in Albania is incremental.[45]

Also, commenting on a League of Nations report on nutrition, T. Zavalani introduces the need for the construction of a database system in Albania, which should be as accurate as that of the League of Nations. He writes: We, who have truly decided to

44 T. Zavalani, Albanian demographic problem, General Remarks, Magazine "Albanian Endeavor", No. 13, January 1938, p.19.

45T. Zavalani, Albanian demographic problem, demographic movement in the years 1931-36, Magazine "Albanian Endeavor", No.14-15, February-March 1938, p. 118.

work on the basis of scientific criteria, should be fully convinced that the first thing we need to do is an inventory of our conditions. In other words, we should complete, as soon as possible, a comprehensive study of our problems, before we decide on how to solve them. Otherwise, every measure we may take will not be able to achieve sustainable results. The improvement of a few details, at a time when the roots of our social wounds remain intact, would only be able to serve as a means of self-delusion.[46]

46T. Zavalani, Report coment League of Nations for food , Magazine "Albanian Endeavor", No.11-12, Tirana, September 1937, pp. 229-231.

III. The Main Representatives of Neo-Albanianism on the Philosophical and Sociological Tradition

General evaluations of philosophy

The main representatives of Neo-Albanian thinking expressed their thoughts on philosophy. Their endeavors resulted in as an assessment of the entire philosophical heritage, often recording the history of values achieved by philosophy. Further, a hierarchy of thoughts was presented which began with Plato and Aristotle and continued with many others, such as R. Descartes, O. Comte, E. Durkheim, E. Kant, A. Schopenhauer, F. Nietzsche, S. Freud, A. Adler, C. G. Jung, H. Bergson, L. Levy-Bruhl, C. Levi-Strauss, and so forth.

The necessity to think in such a broad scope is related to Neo-Albanianism's creed to disseminate culture throughout Albania, to encourage the process of Albanian cultural growth and to complete their intellectual makeup. Moreover, their creed further necessitated their orientation to such in the conditions when, in the labyrinth of a plurality of philosophical systems and the old and new confrontations between them, Albanians would orientate themselves toward systems that were not valid or positive for them.

B. Merxhani defines his opinion as follows: ...for an entire century, the issue of the future destiny of philosophy in the case of a perfect progress of the sciences has been an important point of conversation, in which almost all scientists and philosophers of recent times have participated. There have been, and there still are, some scientists who have come to the conclusion that, one day, science is supposedly going to extirpate philosophy entirely. There have been, and there still are, a good number of other scientists who declare that no scientific perfection scale could ever eradicate, or even damage, the special place that philosophy possesses among the sciences of the mind... The development of new vital formations will always create new philosophical forms. Without ideas (i.e. without diverse and opposing convictions), without struggles between ideas, it has never been possible, nor will it ever be possible, to achieve any new thing in this world.[47]

In the philosophical presentations of the main representatives of Neo-Albanianism one may discern a conception that is related to its classical treatment, which possesses in its composition their views in the area of cognition, metaphysics, ethics, philosophy of history, philosophy of sciences,[*] philosophy of thought, philosophy of life, and so on.

Philosophical Anti-Conformism is not a Misunderstanding or Misinterpretation

From a philosophical perspective, the main proponents of Neo-Albanianism based their solutions on the historical achievements of philosophy and, naturally, made some distinctions, according to their specific preferences. In general, their preferences did not emerge as an extreme differentiation between theories, systems, or different representatives, but as an evaluation of the validity of each one of them in order to assist the achievement of the mission they had set before themselves for the cultural and intellectual elevation of Albanians.

Defining its own position as a view of a nonpolitical—because, according to Neo-Albanians, Albanian people were to be prepared intellectually first, and only then could they enter into politics), intellectual, and illuminating character, Neo-Albanianism, through the voice of B. Merxhani in his March 1937 article "Why I am not a Marxist," expresses some of its preferences for the European philosophy oriented toward

47B. Merxhani, Life and books, Magazine "Albanian Endeavor", No. 4-5-6, March 1937, p. 271.

** philosophy of science:The study of the inner Logic of , according to "The Fontana Dictionary of Modern Thought", pp. 559-560.

democracy, as well as the main aspects of their disagreements with the Marxist doctrine.

Advocating a view that tends towards an equilibrating position, Merxhani expresses his own preferences in the philosophical realm. He also does this to avoid misunderstandings among intellectuals, as well as to express a kind of limited conceptual level of the administration of the state press of the time. He writes: I fear lest some dangerous confusion is generated simply because of the infantile aberrations of some (fortunately) very few, pseudo-intellectuals, or because of the very limited conceptions that (unfortunately) state functionaries usually show in such occasions.[48]

One of the most illustrious intellectuals and writers of the 1930s, P. Marko, esteemed B. Merxhani as one of the most thorough intellectuals of his day and, undoubtedly, as the best publicist during those years. Evaluating the "Albanian Endeavor" and the "Hylli i Dritës" (Light Star) magazines, P. Marko deems them the best cultural, scientific and historical magazines published in that time, when, with great struggle and much labor, Albania was awakening, thus fully affirming the unusual dimension of the Albanian spirit, as well as its indisputable talent and creativity. [49]

It is worth emphasizing that, because he possessed a contemporary educational and philosophical makeup, B. Merxhani tended to bring to the fore the positivist sides of philosophy, under the example of the positivist philosophy of O. Comte and tended to rate sociology highly in the scientific hierarchy.

We, however, are of the opinion that his creed (and that of Neo-Albanianism), in which he gave the dimensions of a set of complex philosophical and sociological views, alongside V. Koça and I Toto, is to be distinguished from Marxist philosophy. This distinction he deemed as highly important, not only for the

---

48B. Merxhani, Why not be Marxist, Magazine "Albanian Endeavor", No. 4-5-6, Tirana, March 1937, pp. 193-196.

49Quoted by the article of L. Stani, Branko Merxhani and "Albanian Endeavor", Newspaper "Light", Tirana 14.02.1993, p.8.

purpose of avoiding misunderstandings, but also in order to give special dimensions to the philosophical creed of Neo-Albanian thinking.

At the time when B. Merxhani was expounding his views, a number of social-philosophical views and systems were being developed in Europe. From a political point of view, the 1930s encompass the emergence and strengthening of the fascist and national-socialist states: in Italy, Mussolini had come to power since 1922; in Germany, Hitler came to power in 1933; in 1936-37, in Spain, the fascist phalanx, led by Franco, rose to power; in Russia the Bolshevik state system was being consolidating. Alongside such states, the system of sustained bourgeois democracies continued to exist within other countries in Europe–such as France and England and in Northern America–the USA.

From the economic point of view, we see the emergence of the 1930s crisis, the most devastating one in humankind's history until today. From the intellectual point of view, a pluralistic climate predominated, with the exception of the countries under fascistic dictatorial regimes, or in the Communist Soviet Union. This is exactly what B. Merxhani had in mind when he writes: ... the present civilized world is divided, not into two, but three, ideological fronts; the third and biggest, most healthy and imposing part remained faithful to the principles of progressive democracy and overcame, with strength and will, all the shaking and unrest caused by the international war of 1914-18 in the social structures of the great peoples that participated in the most terrible battle the history of humankind has ever experienced. And I am convinced that the civilized peoples, those peoples molded and grown within a long tradition of cultural development, can never sacrifice, for the sake of a catastrophic incident (as is every military battle), their cherished and sacred liberties for the possession of which entire worlds have, generation by generation, poured the most noble part of their blood. This is my unshakable conviction.[50]

As thorough experts of diverse philosophical systems, understanding the need for a wider communication of the

---

50Ibid., p. 194.

Albanian thought with the intellectual development in Europe, it seems that Neo-Albanians do not prefer a single particular system or theory. At the most, they are of the opinion that both one, and the other, is necessary. We think that they also appreciate the anti-conformism shown by positivism with its aims to change the nature of philosophy in order to bring it from its conception as a foundation to an instrument of sciences.

The views of the main proponents of Neo-Albanianism revolve around a philosophical conception that aims at summating the theory of cognition, metaphysics and ethics. Furthermore, its proponents view philosophy in every form of the intellectual activity also as a philosophy of science, history, religion, arts, and so on. Neo–Albanianism treats philosophy in its definition as a critical philosophy, as well as a speculative philosophy; it is also called a judgment of thought. This way, philosophy is separated and differentiated from the diverse kinds of thought into specific parts or aspects that precipitate in science, history, and so on. When philosophy is treated as metaphysics, it is better referred to as a critical investigation of the kinds of knowledge, as assertions and methods of thought that create a general view of the world (one might say, a worldview). For this reason, philosophy is viewed as a thought, view, and judgment of thought, and it is thus excluded and differentiated from the many others kinds of thinking. In such a way, their difference is achieved more fully and the position of philosophy is defined, in our view, as well as its ideas, methods and constitution of the object it tries to achieve.[51]

"Cogito, ergo sum**" and the World outside Man

The importance of dealing with this issue comes, according to some of the main representatives of Neo-Albanianism, from the rapports that the individual creates with the reality outside of

----

51See Magazine " Illyria ", No. 1, 2 March, 1934, pp. 11-13.

**** cogito, ergo sum(lat.)-I think, therefore I am(Descartes).

them, a reality that changes in essence according to individual's nature. According to B. Merxhani, the world starts from "the Ego". Here is how he presents this view: My 'Ego' does not have a face. It is not an object that belongs to me. It is a continuation and a collection of all the Egos of the people who have lived on this earth in the past, and harbingers of all those who will come in the future... Inside ourselves we hold alive all who have lived, our dead, and may even hold within us everything that our descendants would enjoy, or will have the ability to enjoy.[52]

In our opinion, this presentation by B. Merxhani also demonstrates an understanding of experience, without leaving unmentioned the complexities that characterize his views. It behooves us to emphasize that this complexity displayed more by B. Merxhani and, generally, somewhat less by the other representatives of Neo-Albanian thinking, is related to their affinities, sometimes in a metaphysical sense and other times in an empirical sense; sometimes in an *a priori* sense and at other times in a materialistic sense. This can be taken as a tendency to grasp a wide gamut of views in this area. In fact, this complexity demonstrates their accommodation to a kind of balance, a kind of *via media* between rational and empirical understanding, which is related to the undefinability of their views within one explanation, as well as to their limited explanatory abilities that bring, as a result, a lack of consistency in their presentations.

Showing frequent affinities with the metaphysical stance regarding cognition, Neo-Albanians introduced, first of all, R. Descartes' analysis, whose examination of the world, or all things that really are, was generally done through rational argumentation, yet also including in this understanding the participation of the direct, or mystical, intuition. R. Descartes saw the world as God's free creation. This view presents the relationship between transcendence and immanence. The notion of transcendence in philosophy is based on that which really is and extends beyond the ordinary wealth of cognition.

52B. Merxhani, Through villages, Magazine "Albanian Endeavor", No. 8, May 1937, pp.65-70.

This transcendent reality is a reality that rises above the human power of cognition. As to God, the transcendent God, according to the theist worldview, is different from an immanent or pantheistic God who is present and knowable by humans. Relying on positivist views concerning the states of the history of humankind, Neo-Albanians in general, and B. Merxhani and V. Koça in particular, thought that the main stages have these specifications: the middle ages began with faith, the modern era with doubt. Here, they give particular importance to the evaluation of R. Descartes' materials in the spectrum of the diverse philosophical theories, when they say: One trend results in empiricism, represented in particular by English thinking (*Bacon*). The other trend results in rationalism, represented by French thinking (*Descartes*). Between these two opposite poles, philosophical speculation vacillated until the two currents met, a century and a half later, within Kantian philosophy.[53]

The presentation – generally *en bloc* – of the philosophical views of Neo-Albanian representatives made on the tercentennial anniversary of publication of R. Descartes's work *Discourse on Method*, which was accompanied by its Albanian translation by V. Koça in the summer of 1937. The aim of this presentation is primarily to give a view of Cartesian values in the history of philosophical thought. But there is also a presence of other philosophers' thoughts, sometimes concerning their views on R. Descartes and, at other times, through the presentation of their own specific views.

According to B. Merxhani, cognition is related to ideas and the actions based on these ideas. Among other things, he writes: But I do not get lost in my own thoughts, because I do not believe them blindly. I trust my actions more. Action is necessary so that we may not lose it; it is necessary so that our thoughts may not be exhausted. [54] It seems that in this author's reasoning, there is a materialist stance that, oftentimes, as if not deliberately, finds its

---

53B. Merxhani, Descartes to us, Magazine "Albanian Endeavor", No. 9-10, August 1937, pp. 137-140 and pp. 200-202.

54B. Merxhani, Through villages, Magazine "Albanian Endeavor", No. 8, May 1937, pp. 65-70.

way into his reasoning, as well as into the reasoning of other representatives of Neo-Albanianism.

Metaphysical Reflections

In presenting these views, generally speaking, the representatives of this thought assess several philosophers and make a selection of those views that they deem reasonable. In this selection, they give their own assessments on ancient Greek philosophy, medieval philosophy, etc. According to them, a feature of these views is the impossibility of cognition, and even the denial of such a problem's existence. Thus, they appreciated G. W. F. Hegel because, according to them, he sees philosophy as a coronation of the long process of collecting, systematizing, classifying and clarifying thought. On the other hand, the philosophical direction that blazed new paths is represented, according to B. Merxhani, by another group of philosophers– the greatest of whom was R. Descartes. *Cogito, ergo sum*, according to New Albanians, shattered the medieval principle of authority– and, with it, the distinctiveness of God's dogma–and gave birth to the new principle of reason.[55]

Many scholars have expressed their appreciation for R. Descartes' philosophy, an appreciation that is brought to the fore by Neo-Albanianism proponents. G. W. F. Hegel, according to B. Merxhani, declared concerning R. Descartes: Descartes is, in fact, the true founder of modern philosophy, for as long as thinking is the latter's principle. The impact of this man on his century and the modern age can never be overestimated. He was a Hero: he took things back to their origins and found afresh the real ground of philosophy to which philosophy went back after losing its way for a thousand years.[56] According to B. Merxhani, assessing R. Descartes' principle, G. Berkeley says: Thinking is the greatest need of our time,[57] while E. Husserl, emphasizes B. Merxhani, gives this evaluation about R. Descartes: ... The

---

55B. Merxhani, Descartes to us, Magazine "Albanian Endeavor", No. 9-10, August 1937, p. 139.

56Ibid., p. 140.

starting point of each philosophy must be sought through a Cartesian-type reflection.[58]

In B. Merxhani's opinion, this catalyst for the turning point in the philosophical realm, R. Descartes was, moreover a descendant of humanism. Humanism was formulated by a Greek scholar, who taught Greek in Florence. This thinker lived in Florence from 1396 on; his name was Manuel Chrysoloras. Furthermore, according to B. Merxhani, R. Descartes has played a great role in the progress of philosophy, especially, through his motto: To do philosophy, we must not believe: we must think![59] B. Merxhani reasons that R. Descartes also opened the way to A. Schopenhauer's philosophical thought, being that the latter called Descartes the father of the new philosophy. This reliance by A. Schopenhauer on R. Descartes, according to this same author, produced the philosophy of voluntarism, which reasons that the world is an image. From this reasoning, Schopenhauer went further and argues that everything that can be imagined, or placed within the framework of cognizance (German, *die Erkenntnis*; French, *la Connaisance*), in other words, all this world, can be reduced to an object related to its subject; it is a mode of view (German, *die Anschauung*) of the thing seen; in other words, a *"die Vorstellung"*–image. An object is not the foundation of the image, but it is equal to it. Nevertheless, this cognizance is not enough. We also want to realize the importance of this image, i.e. we ask if this world is, or is not, an image, and if it is, what is it? "Life," says A. Schopenhauer "is nothing but a *"suffering."* It is an endeavor that is never satisfied. Salvation is but one thing: denial – denial of the will of life. Love is nothing but mercy.[60]

57B. Merxhani, Descartes to us, Magazine "Albanian Endeavor", No. 9-10, August 1937, p. 140.

58Ibid., p. 139.

59B. Merxhani, Who is Descartes?, Magazine "Albanian Endeavor", No. 9-10, August1937, pp. 141-150.

60 Ibid., p.150.

According to B. Merxhani, these diverse ways of philosophizing have their origins in R. Descartes' metaphysics. Furthermore, R. Descartes presents the issue according to the following platform: Are my ideas, which are as certain as my own ways of thinking, real images that represent some different reality from my own self?[61] In our opinion, this exhibits the first component of R. Descartes' metaphysics, which includes *primarily* the being–the concrete possessors of time and space –and, *secondly*, the thoughts and states that are conceived in a dualistic way in time, but not in space and, *thirdly*, the abstract, or universal, entities.

Relying on this reasoning, we would like to point out that R. Descartes presents a complete structure of the world. Then, the issue remains to be solved as to whether this is a mechanistic and deterministic system. Does it consist of chance events, or is it an emergence caused by something inexplicable? B. Merxhani is not able to explained this, so he says: The work of science consists in replacing these appearances with a system, in which no objection will find space.[62] If we view things from this perspective, if we view the world this way, then we will be released from all objections which I–B. Merxhani– fit under the name *"idealisme vulgaire"*–vulgar idealism. However, a more metaphysical objection still remains, viz.: perhaps even the world of science is nothing but a creation or, better yet, a chimerical construct of reason.[63]

There is also another author, N. Peshkëpia, who expresses his opinion on the presentation of the forms of being. He attempts to expound a historical treatment by starting with Aristotle's view, which says: ... Time is the relative number of movement, when this movement represents a part that continues, or ends.[64] The

---

61 According to T. V. Charpentier, Metaphysics of Descartes, Magazine "Albanian Endeavor", No. 9-10 August 1937, f. 151.

62 B. Merxhani, Who is Descartes, Magazine "Albanian Endeavor", Nr. 9-10, August 1937, p. 154.

63 Ibid., p. 154.

64N. Peshkëpia, Mistery of time, Magazine "Albanian Endeavor", No. 11-12, September 1937, p. 251.

ordinary notion concerning the subjective experience of appearance is presented through the example of the ancient Greek who, when asked. *What is time?* —would point to Saturn's statue, full of muscular and holding a sickle in his hand, and would say: "It is called 'chronos' and it regulates the meaningless passage of the days of our life."

According to N. Peshkëpia, a feature of the medieval period (which was characterized by the religious explanation of things) is the separation of the conditions that are the result of God's action and those that are the result of indifferent conditions, in other words those that do not have God's hand" upon them and on which, as a result, no judgment can be made. According to N. Peshkëpia, Christian theology admits that between a perfect condition and nothing, both of which bring about the non-existence of time, the latter is a characteristic and privilege of our real world.

Thus, A. Augustine gives the following answer to the question, what is time? "If you don't ask me, I know it, but if you were to ask me, I couldn't explain it."[65] Apparently, A. Augustine's view fits among the early treatments within the Christian faith, and it vacillates between the definition of the particularity of God's dogma for the explanation of the causality of being and the impossibility of cognizance, between being and non-being, or the unification of both these states.

The above-mentioned author also presents examples in order to explain his understanding of time and human experience. In our opinion, there are two specific examples that relate to conceptual time and the relativity of experiencing flow and continuation of time, as well as with perceptive time.

The first is the story of Friar Felix who, enchanted by the nightingale's song, sat listening to it for a hundred years and, being thus detached from human life, existed in a time that flowed differently from the time of the other people. According to N. Peshkëpia, upon returning to the monastery the friar died as soon as he understood that he had lived on a different time flow

---

65N. Peshkëpia, Mistery of time, Magazine "Albanian Endeavor", No. 11-12, September 1937, p. 252.

than that of ordinary human beings. *The second* is the story of Count Boniface who experienced an entire love affair during the very short time that his king, Frederic, washed his hands. These examples, in our opinion, contain both the fantastic images of the tales and the human endeavor to grasp the immensity of time in conjunction with human pain, which is so finite in relation to infinity.

The author refers to A. Einstein's theory, more for the purpose of giving his assessment the air of the scientific world, despite the fact that he cannot rise to the level of understanding this theory. In this way, he tries to find a link between the events as expressions of the evolution of their understanding and the changes that have occurred in the subjective treatment of time within us, and outside us.

As a result, time's specific subjective flow cannot be outside objective-subjective conceptions. According to N. Peshkëpia, A. Einstein's merit as follows: With his theory, this man–A. Einstein, opening the curtain that covered the window behind which time exists, invites us to see now a world almost completely new, a more coordinated, simpler, more unified, very coherent time, regulated by an unshakable harmony. [66] According to N. Peshkëpia, with A. Einstein's theory, everything that had shrouded time in mystery has now been cut away and time has become well-understood and well-distinguished. We would like to add that we see Einstein's own view as completed in the following definition: namely, space teaches matter how to move, and matter teaches space how to bend.

According to P. S. Laplace (whom N. Peshkëpia takes into consideration), the concept of time is derived from experience, indeed from a successful experience that is presented as an impression, that is subjective and reflects a continuous state of movements that remains and leaves in our mind the continuity of the being of this movement. The presentation of E. Kant's view is characterized by the demonstration of the subjective nature not only of space, but also of time itself.

---

[66] N. Peshkëpia, Mistery of time, Magazine "Albanian Endeavor", No. 11-12, September 1937, p. 251.

According to N. Peshkëpia, E. Kant says: Time and space are also in subjective existence and, for this reason, nor are they visible or outside objects, but only forms of the spirit. Thus, in reality, they do not exist[67].

Thus E. Kant's views is relate to the *object in itself* and its conception as *Noumena*, which are unknowable through empirical observation. According to E. Kant's conception, the things that are located and lie in our experience are a result of the interaction between the physical world and our mental state; these are *phenomena* in the outer and inner sense, and they, in themselves, are not objects of possible experience.

N. Peshkëpia expounds upon H. Spencer's view, which opposes E. Kant's thought. According to N. Peshkëpia, H. Spencer considers E. Kant's idea an absurdity, because he thinks that our consciences tell us that time and space are not in our spirit, but outside it. Hence they are not unintelligible and lie in the kingdom of the unknown. All this reasoning leads N. Peshkëpia to the conclusion that time and space remain a mystery.[68]

It is obvious that this conclusion, reached by N. Peshkëpia, is related to the absence of orientation concerning individual conceptions on space and time, but also to the general notion of categories, and here, the scale of abstraction from individual characteristics is what also achieves the meaning for the new forms of their emergence. N. Peshkëpia connects this absence with the place that past experiences take in cognizance when he says: … in feeling, as well as in perception, it has a single character and distinguishes for us a past object from a present object: the former object is more turbid, less distinguishable, less exact; in a few words, concerning that past object, we have lost the sense of its complexity.[69]

67N. Peshkëpia, Mistery of time, Magazine "Albanian Endeavor", No. 11-12, September 1937, p. 251.

68N. Peshkëpia, Mistery of time, Magazine "Albanian Endeavor", No. 11-12, September 1937, p. 251.

69N. Peshkëpia, Mistery of time, Magazine "Albanian Endeavor", No. 11-12, September 1937, p. 252.

N. Peshkëpia evaluation is different from that presented by B. Merxhani, who, relying more on R. Descartes mixes empiricism with rationalism. We think that Merxhani's view tends to be more *a priori* in nature, namely, that thoughts arise upon direct or indirect experience and, at the least; every event has a cause that is defined in space and time, but only when exclusively defining thought as human reason.[70]

If we further address B. Merxhani's analysis of truth, we shall better present his view. As reported by him: According to us at the Endeavor–*he is referring to the "Albanian Endeavor" magazine*, truth is not found haphazardly. Truth is a quiet and gentle spirit, which is born to be sought after, conversed on, clarified, and continues to be alive for as long as there are people who truly honor and pursue it.[71]

This conclusion is formulated in a polemic by the *"Light Star"* magazine, in order to distinguish the Neo-Albanian view from the religious Catholic view of truth. In general, we would say that the Neo-Albanian conception of cognizance is completely distinguishable from the religious conception in terms of its starting point and the constituent elements of a cognizant nature, but also in terms of its highly social reflection in relation to the individual concrete actions and man's individual experience, where both time and space take on the instrumental value. B. Merxhani begins with the formula "Mind puts matter into motion", and accepts the Bergsonian principle of vitalism or *élan vital*. While L. Skëndo reasons that knowledge is a bizarre feast, its master desires that everyone may come and participate in that fabulous banquet.[72]

70Comp. B. Merxhani, Through Villages, Magazine "Albanian Endeavor", No. 8, May 1937, pp. 65-70.

71B. Merxhani, Polemics with magazine "Light Star", Magazine "Albanian Endeavor", No. 4-5-6, March 1937, p. 248.

72L. Skëndo, The History of Albania, Magazine "Albanian Endeavor", No.. 4-5-6, March 1937, pp. 229-231.

On the Logical Relations of Scientific Knowledge

In terms of the philosophy of science, the Neo-Albanian stance tends toward the study of the inherent logic of science, or the sciences, and by this we mean that they try to present such logic as an important element. Its importance is defined, outwardly, by the objective that Neo-Albanianism presents as its own duty; outwardly, in order to find cohesion in this logic of sciences, the connection that would permit them to achieve the goal they had set before themselves.

From this perspective, we will evaluate two elements of the analysis in the framework of the philosophy of science. *Firstly*, the issue of values, dimensions and structure in scientific theory and the connection with the phenomena and events in the world outside the people and outside their thinking. *Secondly*, the issue of the veracity of scientific theories and laws, relying on the relationships between conclusions and the number of experiments carried out in order to prove, or disprove, the veracity of such conclusions.

In general, representatives of this thought speak for a spectrum of sciences; they evaluate specific facets of a great number of sciences—or sciences in their entirety. These evaluations are less oriented toward natural sciences, mainly biology and physiology, and more toward social sciences, such as sociology, history, psychology, economy, pedagogy and the science of philosophy. When they speak in relation to natural sciences, the representatives of this thought primarily make a summary of their achievements, which have had an influence in the development of humankind from the biological and physiological viewpoint, as well as in the social realm. Here, they allude to the works of R. Descartes, J. Locke, J. Dewey, and W. James in these sciences or to those experiments that they completed in order to present and verify their hypotheses. A number of achievements in the biological and physiological sciences are given, which have had an impact on the qualitative development of the human brain.

As maintained by S. Treska, biology and physiology have yielded wide-ranging materials that have helped–especially psychologists–to make progress in the explanation of the phenomena that are related to the human brain and behavior. According to him, biology has provided three facts for the explanation of such *phenomena*: the enlargement of the brain's hemisphere mass in comparison to the other species of the mammal class, the lengthening of the infancy period in humans in comparison to other living forms, and the established importance of the brain as an organ of thought.[73] Furthermore, these human phenomena prove that adaptability is not something forced from the outside, but is an indicator of the level of development that the human mind has achieved and an indicator for distinguishing man from the animal world. He speaks about the role of the brain and the developments it has undergone from the biological perspective; these developments have widened the number of mental operations by becoming the central organ of thinking in man.

In his opinion, changes have also occurred in the neural system, or in the plasticity of the brain. This plasticity–quality of human brain–begins before birth and continues until the age of eighteen.[74] From a physiological perspective, S. Treska asserts that the qualitative changes that occur make it possible for the neural energy to act on the special centers of the brain, assisting the mind to acquire knowledge from its surrounding environment.[75]

Truth - A Quiet and gentle Spirit

In terms of epistemology, the treatises of Neo-Albanian proponents are related primarily to the theories of dualism, where R. Descartes's thought is the most frequent. The beginning of R. Descartes's thought is *"Cogito, ergo sum,"* which serves as the basis for the expounding of dualism in the aspect of the spirit-body rapport, where spirit appears as reason, as conscience, and the body exists as a separate entity.

73S. Treska, Biology and Education, Magazine "Albanian Endeavor", No. 13, Tirana, Janauary 1938, pp. 13-18, Nr. 14-15, February-March 1938, pp. 119-124.

74S. Treska, Biology and Education, Magazine "Albanian Endeavor", No.13, Tirana, January 1938, pp. 13-18, No. 14-15, Febryary-March 1938, pp. 119-124.

75Ibid., also see S. Treska, Physiology and Education Magazine "Albanian Endeavor", No. 18-24, Tirana, December 1938, pp. 369-375.

According to Neo-Albanians, on the basis of the rational evidence criterion, there is a fundamental difference between thought or spirit, on one side, and the physical being, on the other. Their stance fits within the interactionist viewpoint, which sees these two realms in cooperation with one another despite their primary distinction. In the same way, R. Descartes saw the existence of the two different realms as not something exclusive- a nation that also exists within epiphenomenalism.

According to Neo-Albanians, R. Descartes questions whether or not ideas exist-which are as certain as an individual's thoughts-as true representations of a different reality, outside the certainty of the self. It emerges that the spheres of "I" and outside "I" are totally different realms and that ideas are the result of the impact of events, of the physical reality impressing itself upon the human organism, first of all, on the brain and the neural system- but which do not exert a causal influence on the body.

Along the lines of the epiphenomenal view, the mental and corporeal events are different by nature, are characterized by regularity, and the events that relate to the body are fully explicable as part of a deterministic system of a physical nature, which is not influenced by causes related to thinking. So, accepting this deterministic nature in its essence, the conclusion is derived that every action and event has its own causes; that is, an action happens because it is supposed to happen and, at this point, we must take into account the conditions and circumstances that constitute natural causes for the events.

We can look at this issue not only in terms of distinction, but also interaction. If it is agreed that, no matter how different in nature, the thought and the body interact, then, in keeping with the Neo-Albanian proponents, we may answer R. Descartes' question by saying that, in order to make this connection, we have the data from our senses and, we have our reason and, further, the acceptance of cognition and, even further, the sciences. Hence, the thinkers of this trend accept that the work of science consist of the replacement of these random phenomena with a logical system, in which all the parts work together and form a coherent whole- a system in which there is no place for opposition.[76]

But, at any rate, according to Neo-Albanianism, even though all vulgar idealistic oppositions are rejected, the metaphysical opposition remains, which emphasizes the difference between the work of science as a creation of reason and thinking and the work of science as an ordering of the concrete physical world. So, despite the explanations, the issue still remains as to what is truth in the philosophical sense and in the sense of the knowledge that is achieved by sciences. They say that truth is a quiet and gentle spirit, born in order to be sought after, conversed about and clarified; what is more, it perseveres-waiting for those people who will earnestly seek it and truly honor it.[77]

Thus, this Neo-Albanian formula is, in essence, similar to R. Descartes' basic formula with its two components: first, the being and, second, man's ability to reason, think, and realize the cognition of reality outside of him, the physical reality, as different from the world of reason and its reality. This notion that is given to truth expresses the need for speculation and the process of the verification of its validity. Even though truth has the calm, wisdom, and presence of verification, the articulation of the conditions of verification and circumstances is needed – namely, the conditions and circumstances which make it true or within which it is true. Thus, we need to demonstrate the rapports that exist between speculation and circumstances. At any rate, truth is discovered by people who establish a relationship of coherence between speculations and conditions, and truth will continue to be sought after and discovered for as long as people look for it in the conditions of the human experience. Truth is found in the basic distinction between thought (or spirit) and body, between the world of the psychical and the physical world, between the certainty of the subjective reality and the object reality outside.

76Quoted by T. V. Charpentier, The Metaphysics of Descartes, Magazine "Albanian Endeavor", No. 9-10, Tirana, August 1937, pp. 151-154.

77Magazine "Albanian Endeavor", No. 4-5-6, Tirana, March 1937, p. 248.

In the presentations of the pragmatist position, primarily in the articles of S. Treska, one may notice a difference from the notion give above. His examination corresponds with the monist physical treatment, which is most often encountered among the natural science. According to the views of the above-mentioned author, all brain phenomena may be summarized in the explanation given by the natural sciences and, primarily, by biology and physiology. However, he tends to favor neutral monism when explaining the body-soul rapport. Thus, he says that thought, in itself, is a specific special construction that may be known through experience.

When thus introduced, this treatment is similar to the classical pragmatist notion of truth. One of the views of the classical presentation of pragmatism is truth as satisfaction, a satisfaction of the faith, which is verified empirically and determines a true supposition in the shape of something that is expected to happen in the way that faith is expected or satisfied.[78]

The Philosophy of History: A Systematizing Reflection

In their analysis of the philosophy of history, the treatises by the main representatives of Neo-Albanianism aim at conceiving a meta-history that constructs a historical system in the form of a regularity of historical events. This presentation helps them define a general line of the events included in Albanian history, as well as provide a critical reflection on their methods of historical study and reasoning. This can be seen in the works of B. Merxhani, V. Koça, L. Skëndo, and the like.

L. Skëndo's theories on the conception of a pure nationalism, which is also an element of Neo-Albanianism, tend toward conceiving meta-history as an auxiliary reflection for the construction of a system of history that would be helpful in accurately achieving and systematizing the history of Albanians.

78A. Bullock & O. Stallybrass, The Fontana Dictionary of Modern Thought, W. C. Sand Co Ltd, London 1977, pp. 491-492.

Such a meta-history would masterfully explain historical events and would present a well-constructed historical system. Yet, more importantly, it would stimulate Albanians to study their history, to get to know themselves and their heroism, ultimately uniting them with one another, increasing their love for the nation and their nationalism.[79]

B. Merxhani, on the other hand, conceives this problem in both its components: as a need for a critical reflection on historical reasoning in general, as well as a complete history of Albania that is valuable for Albanians. *Firstly*, such a conception must avoid the chaos that exists in Albanian society concerning history, alongside the chaos concerning other issues. *Secondly*, it should eliminate the negative elements of Albanian life, which have prevented a correct evaluation of Albanian history and its most crucial events. In fact, it is necessary, from the point-of-view of Neo-Albanian thinking, to find a national philosophy, a national morality and a national education.

B. Merxhani argues that, for the successful construction of a historical system, it is necessary to avoid traditions. According to him, traditions exist because of accidental conclusions and, thus, should only be accepted as symbols that can be changed as desired. By accepting the subjective stance and the speculative tendency, such a treatment of traditions is introduced that, if their existence and influence are deemed unnecessary, then society can arbitrarily claim the deficiency of these traditions.[80]

Culture, in general, helps define the correct method of historical reasoning. Culture achieved the existence and a complete development. Ultimately, the duty lies in constructing a scientific history while relying on culture, and in creating museums, libraries, archives, and other such institutes of cultural preservation.[81] Moreover, part of the conception of history is the

---

79L. Skëndo, The History of Albania, Magazine "Albanian Endeavor", No.4-5-6, Tirana, March 1937, pp. 229-231.

80B. Merxhani, Tradition and national Idea, Magazine "Illyria", 17. 12. 1935, p. 5.

81B. Merxhani, Politics and Culture, Magazine "Albanian Endeavor", No.2, Tirana, November 1936, pp. 70-71.

presentation of views and the selection of the best model among them—specifically, the model that would be deemed most valuable for Albania. This is done in order to give life to processed philosophical views, which serve as guides for societal reforms.

On the basis of this concept, the need for philosophical refinement extends even to the stimulation of social reforms. For this reason, it is necessary to avoid dogmatism, thus creating space for these advanced social reforms, and these changes ought to happen in the social realm. Nevertheless, as indicated by Neo-Albanian proponents, an intermediate state is needed in between the state of refining social views and the state of their achievement in society. This intermediate state is needed in order to achieve the general thought, the general conclusions on the country's level of development, bearing in mind that the issues are related to the past, to the country's development at the time, and with the cultural and intellectual level of Albanians. Deficiencies existed in their concepts of society and its institutions; according to V. Koça, the people had the qualities of passive, amorphous matter.[82]

Neo-Albanians, in general, think that the specification of realistic programs for social changes and reforms is necessary. But, as stated by B. Merxhani, Neo-Albanians were not prophets.[83] Bringing to light the differences between their notion of the nature and the elements of social reforms and those of other conceptions, especially those of Marxism, B. Merxhani underlines that the economy did not hold a privileged position in society and *social phenomena* is often the cause of economic developments.[84]

In the endeavor to find the most accurate philosophical theories as a basis for valuable and successful social reforms, representatives of this thinking discover some affinity between the views of K. Marx and E. Durkheim. The likeness between K.

82Magazine "Illyria", 25. 03. 1934, p. 1.

83Magazine "Albanian Endeavor", No. 25-27, Tirana, January-March 1939, p. 9.

84Newspaper "Demokratia", 30. 07. 1932, p. 3.

Marx and E. Durkheim rests in their evaluation of social movements as the result of natural causes and their assertion that life issues, as well as issues of the spirit, submit to natural laws.[85] In this, both philosophers were valuable in the eyes of Neo-Albanian thinkers.

It is necessary that social reforms, which Neo-Albanianism deems as generally reasonable, be orientated toward solving the moral and psycho-synthetic issues; in other words, they ought to be developed within purely nationalistic and democratic frameworks.[86] Social reforms must bear in mind the individual, opposing and rejecting leftist philosophical theories, which tended toward reforms of a general social nature. This, in our opinion, categorizes Neo-Albanians into the methodological individualism within the philosophy of history; their thinking is related to the idea that all of the collective phenomena of an individual—which emerge as the actions, interactions, goals, hopes, and thoughts of the person—adjust according to the traditions created by this individual.

B. Merxhani opines that such individualism must also be achieved in Albania, and this would be a sign of the progress and the high level of development within the civilized world.[87] Providing arguments for the need of social reforms, in general, the proponents of this thought claim that they must be implemented part by part, also including competition as an element of the qualitative development of society in the capitalist manner and as a real demonstration of the capabilities of the individual.

85Magazine "Illyria", 19. 11. 1935, p. 5.

86Magazine "Illyria", 12. 11. 1935, p. 3.

87B. Merxhani, Individualism, Magazine "Albanian Endeavor", No.7, Tirana, April 1937, pp. 13-16.

Endeavors for the Sociological Study of Albanian Reality and of the Individual-Society Rapport

The main representatives of Neo-Albanian thinking deem sociology as indispensable for Albania and the Albanians, as well as for the fulfillment of the spectrum of developed sciences in Albania. In the conception of sociology, B. Merxhani's view is particularly conspicuous. Relying on strict methodological criteria, such as the construction of the science of sociology, he assumes this undertaking not only for scientific purposes, but also bearing in mind Albania's need for a developed sociological thought.

Viewing sociology as an important element of the positive sciences, B. Merxhani also looks at it as a presentation of the way in which it was developed, and he expounds upon the methodology that sociology uses for the explanation of the function of society from its specific perspective. He achieves this by delineating a scheme of the sociological examination, which expresses not only the relation between the basic sociological concepts but, at the same time, forecasts the instruments that serve to achieve the structure of sociological thinking.

Here, below, is the schematic presentation of O. Comte's and B. Merxhani's views:

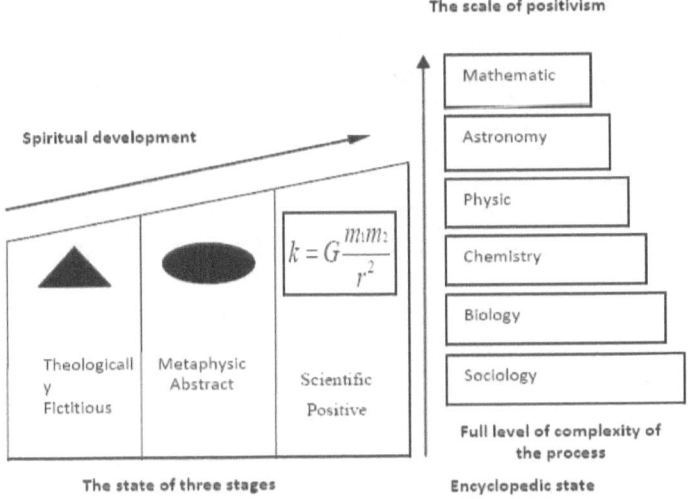

Fig.1. Presentation of O. Comte's Views (Resource: DTV Atlas zur Philosophie, München 1991).

This can compare with thought of Neo-Albanians

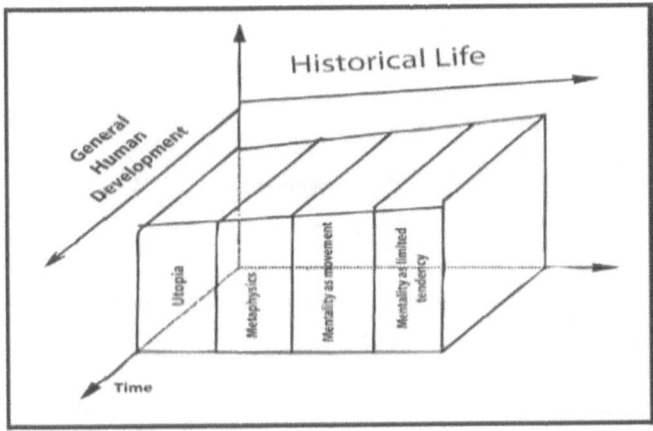

Fig.2. Presentation of Societal Development in B. Merxhani's "Civic Man" (created by I. Nikaj)

As can be seen from the schemes above, the difference between O. Comte's and B. Merxhani's notions is that O. Comte believes that, from the viewpoint of methodology and veracity, sociology is the most complete science, while B. Merxhani holds the opinion that this is not true; in fact, according to B. Merxhani, there is no science that is able to solve every difficulty simply by using O. Comte's magical key.[88] On the other hand, according to Dh. Shuteriqi, science formulates the leading conceptions which study the human mind: namely, the ideas of cause, space, number, bodies, life, conscience, and society. All of these basic ideas are continually developed, because they are the final summary of all scientific work, without being its starting point. Nevertheless, science is a collective work, because it has been constructed through the cooperation of scholars of all times.[89]

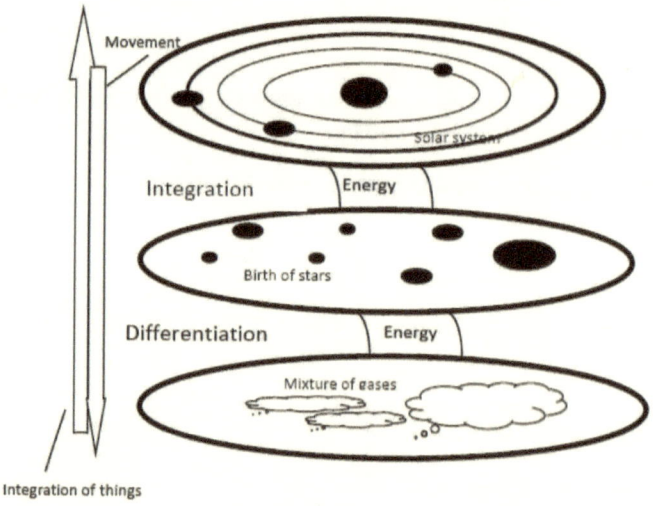

Fig.3. Development according to Spencer (example: The Birth of a Solar System) (Resource: DTV Atlas zur Philosophie, München, 1991)

88B. Merxhani, Comte and contemporary Sociology, Magazine "Albanian Endeavor", No. 16, Tiranë, April 1938, pp. 185-187.

89Magazine "Albanian Endeavor", No. 17, Tiranë, May 1938, pp. 277-282.

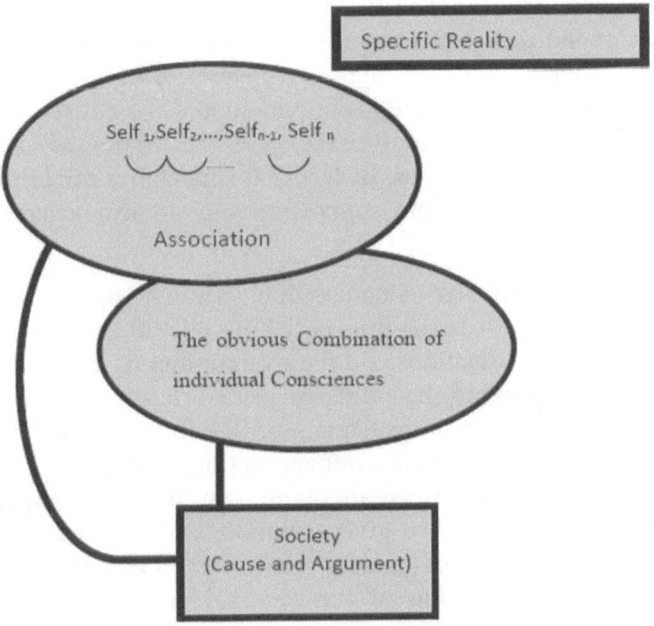

Fig.4. E. Durkheim's View on Social Interaction (created by I.Nikaj)

In light of E. Durkheim's scheme about the concept of society, we may understand what he means when he says that society is not a simple collection of individuals, but a system formed by their association, which represents a specific reality (*rèalite spècifique*) and has its specific characters. Undoubtedly, no collective thing can be achieved in the absence of particular consciences: yet, even this indispensable condition is inadequate; something else is also needed: these consciences must be associated (*associe*) and interrelated; in fact, they are to be interrelated in an obvious way. This interrelation is what produces social life and also explains it.[90]

90Ibid., p. 282.

While O. Comte says there is no individual without a society, E. Durkheim adheres to this view within his scheme of the sociological concept. For B. Merxhani, our historical condition, produces individualism; negative force that does not contribute to the improvement of the conscience level in general. In Merxhani's thought, the Ego-individual and the entirety of Egos constitute the past, the present, and the future of society.[91] According to him, the goal of Neo-Albanianism is the creation of a mental life and of the supporting sociological principles of national life.[92]

According to him, Neo-Albanian doctrine, in all its logical plans, programs and draft-laws, aims enriching this rule, is attaining the perfection of its functions and the overcoming of its turbulences, as well as improving the ruling of justice, laws, and peace. Not the state as such, but the state's social feeling is the moving power of every essential human action,[93] because Albanian society was in an intermediary stage between the governance of the collective order and a given solution, which relied on power. The former represented society, while the latter represented the state.[94] For the creation of the national consciousness, which relied on the tribal and religious consciousness, sociology was of great necessity.[95] From a sociological perspective, the state represents a summary of the moral, scientific, artistic, religious and juridical personality of the human crowd.[96] The state is a supra-class instrument for the disciplining of the masses, as well as a force and fist to exercise its will on the egotistic dispositions of the individuals.[97]

91Ibid., No 8, Tirana, May 1937, pp. 65-70.

92Newspaper "Demokratia", 08. 12. 1928.

93Magazine "Illyria", 18. 03. 1934, p. 1.

94Ibid, p.1.

95Magazine"Illyria", 14. 03.. 1936, p. 2.

96Newspaper"Demokratia", 01. 01. 1929, p. 5.

97Newspaper Demokratia, 08. 01. 1929, p. 5.

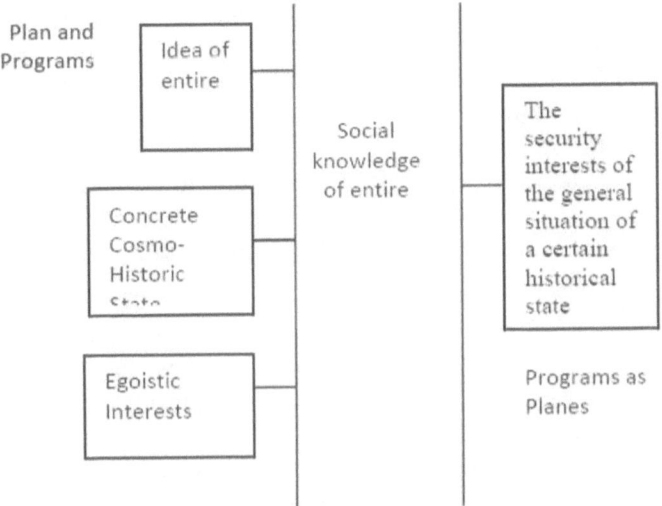

Fig.5. Schematic Presentation, as Portrayed by B. Merxhani, of the Social Cognition of the Concrete Cosmos-Historical Condition.1(Created by I. Nikaj)

Endeavors were made by the most distinguished proponents of Neo-Albanianism to give their own notion of the individual-society rapport. This is a well-treated issue but, in our opinion, also left unresolved. This treatment should have included issues that related to the structure, the organization of society, and the political institutions, which interrelate within the individual-society rapport. Realistically, in society, all forms of association have identifiable structures that permit the analysis and definition of their elements, as well as the way they operate together during their existence as an entirety within the structures. Certainly, the elements of structure are either clearly or covertly related to their functions.

The preeminent idea regarding the individual-society rapport within Neo-Albanianism is demonstrated through the treatments of O. Comte and E. Durkheim. However, it is often unified with another rapport that is not analogous to the first in all of its dimensions and elements. By this we mean the difference between the individual-society rapport and the individual-nation rapport. When they appear as advocates of O. Comte's view, their conceptions move within the statics and dynamics explained by this thinker. The distinguishing of O. Comte's thinking is the treatment of the interaction between the individual and society- in manner given by physics; in other words, masses acting to conditions of statics and dynamics. Naturally, there exists a collusion of thoughts and this is due to the fact that it is not clear where the difference lies between O. Comte's view on the interaction between statics and dynamics and Neo-Albanians views.

The endeavor of the most distinguished proponents of Neo-Albanianism, such as B. Merxhani and V. Koça, has been very important in bringing this issue to light. Besides this, Neo-Albanianism makes a comparison of views but does not take a clear position, nor does it evaluate all of the views. One may have the impression that, because he clearly quotes E. Durkheim's thought, B. Merxhani considers E. Durkheim to be correct.

In one of the pages of the "Albanian Endeavor" magazine, we find this thought by E. Durkheim: "Society is not a simple collection of individuals, but a system formed by their association, which represents a specific reality (*rèalite spècifique*) and has its specific characters. Undoubtedly, no collective thing can be achieved in the absence of particular consciences, but even this indispensable condition is inadequate; something else is also needed: these consciences must be associated (*associes*) and interrelated; in fact, they are to be interrelated in an obvious way. This interrelation is what produces social life and also explains it."[98]

We think that these explanations are not very complete if we bear in mind that the analysis of society made by the main proponents of Neo-Albanianism does not fully the issues of the individual-nation rapport. Now we may explain in a concise way what is problematic in this treatment.

---

[98] Magazine "Albanian Endeavor", No. 17, Tiranë, May 1938, p. 253.

First of all, the treatment of this issue from the sociological viewpoint sets out to contradict O. Comte. In an article entitled "Comte and Contemporary Sociology," published in issue No. 16 of the "Albanian Endeavor," the author, B. Merxhani, does not hesitate to reject O. Comte's view and to take an agnostic position when he says that "humankind does not consist of a single human society that walks on a correct and unilateral development." This happens because, according to B. Merxhani, "there is no single human society as such, but only a group of diverse individualities."[99] This perspective demonstrates a number of differences between societies in relation to the level of their development and exhibits societies that have their own particularities; namely, their particularities rest in the main components of their political institutions and in the different psycho-sociological levels of the individuals (see Fig. 6).

Second of all, despite the similar elements that appear in the views of the most distinguished proponents of Neo-Albanianism, their merit is that, in general, concerning this specific issue, they not only departed from Marxism, but also tried to polemicize against it. It is another issue whether this polemic was well-argued or not, and how well they were able to oppose that theory with strong arguments. Along these lines, the most representative article is that by B. Merxhani with title "Why I am Not a Marxist," published in issues No. 4, 5, and 6 of the "Albanian Endeavor" in March 1937.

In this article, from the social-political perspective, B. Merxhani sees as ungrounded Marxism's claim that two-thirds of the people's profits go into the hands of one-fifth of a country's population. He also sees as unfair and unfounded the claim that the capitalist regime destroys light industry and rejects Marxist assertion that the capitalists' profits constantly increase, while the workers' wages decrease. Moreover, according to B. Merxhani, it is impossible for individuals of uncultured strata to solve the issues of society in a democratic way. This author expresses himself as follows: If the worker is really in a miserable plight, then this condition may have only one effect:

99B. Merxhani, Comte and contemporary Sociology, Magazine "Albanian Endeavor", No. 16, Tirana, April 1938, pp. 185-187.

misery will become an ideology and the revolutionary current of the proletariat will go on rising. Yet, how could a miserable proletarian be able to achieve the lofty duties with which Marx charges him? Misery can only give birth to a single thing: misery.[100]

Researcher G. Bobi, in his study "Cultural Paradox," defines the main proponents of Neo-Albanian thinking as radical and disciplined democrats, based on the definitions that they have given about themselves. He defines the Neo-Albanians' creed as an endeavor to oppose Marxism from a practical perspective and to strengthen patriotism. Here is how this researcher evaluates the merit of Neo-Albanian thinking: In order not to dwell any further on presenting the 'views' of 'the disciplined democrats' on diverse issues of Albanian culture and society, we say that, concerning their statements for the creation of a 'mental movement' whose aim was the 'description,' 'classification,' and 'concentration' of all the issues that are related to the 'specific structure' of the Albanian society, in order to thus create, 'not a literary-romantic Albanianism,' but a 'radical-democratic Albanianism,' 'neo-Albanians' were truly disciplined 'to move something essentially ahead in the Albanian life and, generally, in the Albanian culture.[101]

Likewise, researcher G. Bobi goes on to explicate worth of the Neo-Albanianism: today, 'they'–their magazines–have the value of cultural 'facts' that speak about a period of very complex, social and historical, circumstances, about a time when Marx, Nietzsche, Descartes, Bergson, Croce, Freud, Jung, Adler, Comte, Weber, Durkheim, Mannheim, Valeria, Pirandello, and many other writers and philosophers, sociologists and scholars had started to express their voice, even if unarticulated, in the Albanian language. This *alali* *[cry] in our culture cannot be left

---

100Magazine "Albanian Endeavor", No. 4-5-6, Tirana, March 1937, p. 196.

101G. Bobi, Cultural Paradox, Rilindja, Prishtina 1986, p. 147.

*' *alali* quoted by D. Kish, A Tomb for Boris Davidovich, f. 11, Tirana, Çabej 1999, given this explanation by translator: from Old French **ha la lit** (alb. *hë, ja ku dergjet*), hue and sign with the hunting horns of deer hunting, which becomes known that the deer had fallen. In our, it used with the meaning of hue; maybe, also, with meaning of voice unarticulated.

unnoticed.[102] As an endeavor in self-discovery, self-knowledge and self-possession, this functional type of the Albanian culture had as its motto: "there is no politics, but only culture." Its most characteristic syntagm: "disciplined democracy." Moreover, it's most active animator: Branko Merxhani. Its main forum: "Albanian Endeavor." Its artistic concretization: Lasgush Poradeci's poetry.[103] So we have a summarized view of what may be called the Neo-Albanians' most valuable qualities.

The Conscious, the Subconscious, and the Truths of the Ego

In the area of psychology, B. Merxhani is again conspicuous as a galvanic element in the methodological and scientific evaluation aspect of psychology. In psychology, he tends to favor S. Freud's psychoanalysis. In general, Neo-Albanians have tried to widely treat psychological issues within this theoretical orientation, which can be clearly evidenced in their research views. The "Albanian Endeavor" especially, there are writings on diverse psychological issues, in fact, in almost every one of its issues.

The Major Methodological Issues Treated by Neo-Albanianism

Firstly, in relation to explaining dreams, S. Freud's method deals with technical interpretation, with a foundation in spiritual determinism. These ideas are apparent in the explanation that S. Freud gives about dreams; that is he concludes that the spiritual life is not only that which is conscious, but also that which is subconscious, real and dynamic. Freud analyzes the elements that constitute dreams alongside the spiritual functions that characterize them. Dreams are a result of suppressed experiences and desires, which are built into the reality of the subconscious

---

102G. Bobi, Cultural Paradox, Rilindja, Prishtina 1986, p.147.

103G. Bobi, Selfcultural Context, Dukagjini, Peja 1994, p. 47

as events. So, because of the existing separation (where the conscious suppresses the subconscious), misunderstandings occur.

The investigation of these understandings reveals a true subconscious, where all the shameful or at any rate, negative tendencies of our daily life are to be found- which were hidden from the conscience when they were suppressed. Nonetheless, these buried tendencies possess enough dynamism to cry out occasionally in a clear way; yet, in most cases, they are covered and deformed as if they are trying to escape our control.[104]

In this framework S. Freud's conception is treated in the creation of psychoanalysis as a general psychological theory, as therapy, and as method. As a theory, it is expounded in both variants: on one hand, in the treatment of the conscious-subconscious rapport, which are viewed as a system. According to this treatment, the system expresses itself in two basic forms: it its most sexual or self-defensive energy in its essence, and the second variant where it takes the form of the aggressive and destructive desire. Psychoanalysis is based on the free associations for the patient who cooperates with the psychoanalyst, who plays the role of an anonymous figure that must avoid any confrontation with the patient. This means that a unique relationship must be created between the patient and the psychoanalyst, whose goal is to until the patient's emotional knot.

As a method, psychoanalysis tries to collect techniques to be used in practice and this is an asserted procedure on the individual level. S. Freud relied on J. Breuer and P. Janet, according to B. Merxhani, for the creation of his own new methodology. Furthermore, Freud refined the theory of the libido's stages of development.[105] According to B. Merxhani, in studying hysteria, S. Freud came to the conclusion that it is the result of the division of intelligence into a duplication of

---

104B. Merxhani, What Psycho-Analysis?, Magazine "Albanian Endeavor", No. 17, Tirana, May 1938, pp. 205-208.

105B. Merxhani, Five lectures on Psycho-Analysis, Magazine "Albanian Endeavor", No. 17, Tirana, May 1938, pp. 283-290.

personality. Through his practical observation of patients with hysteria, Freud noticed that opposition exist; in other words, within the diseased, the power of the conscious and the subconscious struggle against one another. Moreover, the function of suppression is present. Then, duplication occurs; the psychical division that the hysteric exhibit is not caused by some kind of innate synthetic inability of their mental mechanism. According Merxhani's explanation of Freud, hysteria reveals its dynamics as a fight between the conscious and the subconscious. And the suppression hypothesis is not the end, but only the beginning, the beginning of his psychological theory. The reaction of the diseased patient is that he admits that he reacted well when he suppressed his desire, but in fact he replaces the automatic mechanism of suppression with a moral judgment. But the truth is that desire may only be fought in the full light of the conscience.[106]

Determinism is defined as the basic element of mental events and B. Merxhani generally explains dreams through this element. According to him, the dream's visible content is a replacement and deformation of latent ideas. This deformation is caused by an opposition or defense on the part of the Ego, which, when awakened, opposes in every way the desires that we have in our subconscious. This opposition is very weak when we are asleep. Furthermore, the phenomenon of dreaming dreams, according to him, is an individual phenomenon and every person who dreams has latent ideas which he does not know about.

According to B. Merxhani, in order to discover what the true content of a particular dream is, we must make latent ideas visible. A dream is the realization of a desire that, for one reason or another, we have not been able to fulfill. The visible content of a dream may be considered a changed realization of our suppressed desires.[107]

106B. Merxhani, Five lectures on Psycho-Analysis, Magazine "Albanian Endeavor", No. 17, Tirana, May 1938, pp. 283-290.

107B. Merxhani, Five lectures on Psycho-Analysis, Magazine "Albanian Endeavor", No. 18-24,Tirana, December 1938, pp.378-385.

IV. Neo-Albanians views on the Nation and State

The Notion of Nation and the Factors of its Formation

The attention of the main proponents of Neo-Albanianism focuses on the discussion of issues related to the nation, the national cause and the national ideals, etc. Relying on O. Comte's views, they view the nation's components in the general framework of the distinctive nature between subject and matter. This concept appears in society, according to O. Comte, in its statics and dynamics; in other words, the elements of the nation are formed in a specific environment and are not defined by matter determinism, but by social determinism.

Based on this view, B. Merxhani reasons that the nation represented the highest, most synchronized expression of collective idealism, the personality of which was not to be found in our bodies, but in our souls.[108] This reasoning is related to E. Durkheim's notions of collective conscience and collective imaginations, which are the result of his belief that society is not a simple sum of individuals that compose it, or of individual consciences, but is born through social actions, within specific collective condition-it is the result of the birth and emergence of new elements in human experience, values, the will and behavior. Furthermore, E. Durkheim regards specific feelings and values related to specific cultural symbols as most distinctive in the collective imagination; the specific cultural symbols correspond to the specific traditions of each culture. In themselves, collective imaginations are a social-cultural heritage that defines the borders of the community's collective life.

Thus, since this definition relates to the way in which the distinctive elements of a certain national entity are realized in

---

108Newspaper "Demokratia", 07.03.1931, p.6.

distinction to another national entity, Neo-Albanianism does consider time and environment as a nation's specific elements but tend toward the spiritual and ideal elements as the most important characteristics of a nation. Considering this stance on the issue of nation, they value, from the historical perspective, tradition and its impact on the formation of the Albanian nation. According to them, this tradition finds its most illustrious periods in the era of Skanderbeg and in the period of National Renaissance. This is so because it is in these periods that the seed of culture was sown and national ideal was formed.[109]

Historical events truly impact the step-by-step creation of those features that, alongside other elements, influence the creation of relationships between the people who live and share the same destiny. Undoubtedly, the era of Skanderbeg constitutes a very important period in the history of Albanian people; whereas, when it comes to defining the historical period when the Albanian nation was conceived, era of Skanderbeg does not fit the bill. Albanian historiography advocates the view that the period of the formation of the Albanian nation coincides with the period of Albanian National Renaissance, approximately in years 1840-1912.

Esteeming culture as an important element that characterizes a nation, Neo-Albanianism expresses the opinion that, within culture, language is the most important. Language realizes national unification, the great literary blooming.[110] According to B. Merxhani, the elements that distinguish one nation from another (in fact, elements of the ideal nation) are language, morality and the usage of the same tools.[111] B. Merxhani's concept tends to value the elements of the spiritual realm for the formation of the nation but also accepts elements of the material realm.

This concept stems from the fact that his general philosophical views cannot be classified within one philosophical system, but

109Newspaper "Demokratia", 21. 06. 1930, p.3.

110Newspaper "Demokratia", 11. 02. 1933, p.3.

111Magazine "Illyria", 02. 11. 1935, p. 5.

are a compound of a number of philosophical components, alongside the adoration he expresses for sociology. This is revealed when he says that environment plays a special role in the formation of a nation's features[112] and, alongside the spiritual components, this environment also includes the material components. In other words, the factors that influence the development of society are that it is not just the ideas, but also the era, the new state of things, and the new conditions of life and its needs - and these exercise a mysterious influence on our ideas and our dispositions.[113] Thus, the formation of a nation's features is also impacted by time, geographical environment, as well as the collection of people, which are viewed more as elements that act as appendixes to the spiritual sphere, and as components that influence the formation of the national ideal. In addition, culture, language, and tradition, are very important aspects in the formation of a nation's features. B. Merxhani gives import to the presence of the ideal; national ideal has as a condition the existence of the society and the social and spiritual life, while he excludes the individual who is connected to the material and substantial life because, according to him, only social life–and not the individual life–could form the ideal, because the individual life only offers material profit.[114]

Starting from such a notion on nature and the components of the nation, they dwell on the conditions that have impacted Albanian history on its road toward the formation of the national ideal, the national consciousness, as well as what is positive for the strengthening of these feelings. This is the reason why proponents of this thinking polemicized against the "Light Star" magazine on the issue of the race to which Albanians belong. In the early studies on the nation, race is evaluated as a component that was present during its formation. But, for the representatives of Neo-Albanianism, as well as for many non-Albanian scholars, this is an argument that was overcome by scientific studies on this issue.

112Newspaper "Demokratia", 17. 06. 1933, p. 3.

113Magazine "Illyria", 01. 07. 1934, p. 2.

114Newspaper "Demokratia", 09. 03. 1929, p.3.

The representatives of Neo-Albanianiasm in general – and B. Merxhani in particular – do not accept the idea that a nation is defined by race. They connect this with the issue of the inter-mixture of people, as the result of the coexistence between those who were invaded by their invaders, and such events were numerous in the period before the formation of nations. Inter-mixtures occur not simply in the patrilineal descendants, but also in the spiritual realm, and in the area of production and in the realm of traditions and customs. According to B. Merxhani, Slavic, Greek, Turkish, Arabic, Cherkess, Italian, French, German, and other kinds of blood run through Albanian veins (!)[115] For this reason, the issue of nation cannot be linked to race, because these are two discrete phenomena that have been distinguished from one-another through time. The inter-mixture of races is a biological and historical issue, which occurred in the earlier periods the human history, and thus a limited phenomenon in the modern age. Moreover, one of the reasons why the issue of inter-mixture no longer presents a problem is that this issue has been solved with the define ability and continuity of existence of the nations- and this is the subtext of the Neo-Albanian thinkers' answer to the "Light Star" magazine.[116]

Neo-Albanianism examines other issues as well, such as, the stance that Albanians have held toward the nation and their national issue and the question of how their nation might preserve its being and continuity. For this, they argue that, throughout their history, Albanians have sometimes shown themselves incapable of solving the problem of their national issue. They attribute this to a kind of backwardness in the general development of Albanian society and to certain elements of the Albanian psychological nature. According to them, backwardness is a result of the Albanians' historical plight in the past, since it suffered from successive invasions, of which the most harmful and the longest was the Turkish invasion.

115Magazine "Illyria", 24. 08. 1935, p. 5.

116Ibid., 09. 02. 1929.

Foreign rule had caused social and historical shocks, thus making it difficult for Albanians to develop. These shocks, according to Neo-Albanians, had primarily influenced language, family, ideas and the social tendencies of the people, as well as the social institutions.[117] According to V. Koça, Albanians have also inherited negative qualities from this historical experience, such as their preoccupation with the material realm and with immediate interests, as well as their sidelining of the causes that were related to the nation and the national ideal.

This backwardness has caused Albanians to possess an ideal that is primitive, sociologically narrow or low, and protoplasmic.[118] Therefore, from the historical perspective, the Albanians' fate has not been the same as that of the other civilized nations of Europe. Albanians had the task of escaping from the chaos in which they found themselves. The representatives of Neo-Albanianism were not the first, nor the last, Albanian thinkers who have pointed out the existence of some rather uninspiring features in the nature of their people. Thus, for example, the renowned Albanian thinker and diplomat, Faik Konica, in his work, *"Albania∇The Rocky Garden of Southeastern Europe,"* defines individualism as a psychical feature of the Albanian character. According to him, "the absence of this spirit in the flock may be interesting, but it has had fatal consequences for Albania's unity."[119]

Viewing the issue from such a perspective, they proposed that O. Comte's *principle-rule-progress* be followed, because the national consciousness would be strengthened. Within this reasoning, they also thought that the elements of the spiritual realm must be changed on the basis of the spiritual determinism concept. Elements of this determinism were language, culture, religion, traditions, and morality.

117V . Nirvana, For a bit of bread, Magazine "Illyria", 11. 03. 1934, p. 1 and Magazine "Illyria", 18. 04. 1936, p. 1.

118ibid.

119F. Konica, "Albania-The rock Garden of Southeastern Europe", Works, "Naim Frashëri", Tirana 1993, p. 423.

Language was viewed as a major means for the unification of Albanians, as well as the axis of their cultural activity. On the other hand, on the basis of the fact that all that Neo-Albanian proponents considered culture as their sphere of action, culture became their main evaluative criterion on the issue of the nation. Their mission looked forward to the synthesis of the national philosophy with the national morality and national education. Without this synthesis, the notion of patriotism could not be realized in Albania.[120] According to B. Merxhani, without culture it is not possible to lay the first stone in the foundation of the nation. Nation means culture, and culture means nation. Those who cannot understand this, are not only unclear on the notion of culture but, at the same time, unconsciously and ignorantly deny the notion of nation. They confuse the meaning of the word culture with the meaning of the word civilization.[121]

In a stage where Albanian society, which according to V. Koça, had not yet formed its nation[122] or, according to B. Merxhani, had formed its nation but was in a kind of intermediate stage of development,[123] the duty of Neo-Albanianism was to help in the cultural development of the country and in the creation of cultural solidarity.

Nation and National Ideal

In the period when Neo-Albanianism proponents carried out their activity, Albania was confronted with complicated foreign and interior issues, the most significant being the economic crisis, the threat of Nazism and Communism and the Second World War. Thus, in order to neutralize their negative effect on the Albanian nation, the strengthening of patriotism and the national consciousness was needed. According to V. Koça, it is

---

120Magazine "Illyria", 26. 11. 1935, p. 5 and 14. 03. 1936, p. 2.

121Magazine "Illyria", 11.01. 1936, p.1.

122V. Nirvana, In the Path of Nationalism, Magazine "Albanian Endeavor", No. 7, Tirana, April 1937, pp.1-7.

123Magazine "Illyria", 18. 03. 1934, p .1.

the duty of the intellectuals to assist in the strengthening of the national consciousness.

As maintained by V. Koça, Albanian patriotism is characterized by anti-Communism, so Communism must be opposed by the national ideal, the energetic ideal, as he calls it, which finds its stimuli in Albania's historical past and in the values and traditions created by it.[124] Accordingly, the heroic spirit of the past will bring spiritual liberty, which will be in the marrow of the energetic ideal. This new spirit must find support in the Albanian youngsters- in a youth nourished with the heroic spirit of the Albanian glorious past- as well as in the renewal of the leading elite. Here, V. Koça is also orientated by social politics, which must give support to the energetic ideal.[125]

Reconciling V. Koça's view with that of B. Merxhani, we notice that they propose two different outlooks on this issue. While V. Koça deems of the Albanian nation's survival as complicated by the conditions created at the time, B. Merxhani sees these conditions as not very unfavorable for the Albanian nation. According to B. Merxhani, the national ideal and the national consciousness must not associate to closely with politics and the governance system. According to him, the important thing is the rapport, the relations, and the continuity of these relations that the individual creates with his nation.[126]

According to B. Merxhani, the activity of Neo-Albanianism tends toward patriotism, which necessarily emphasize the common elements between patrilineal or tribe descent, the common language, and the historical ties among people who belong to a certain nation or who live in a specific territory. In general, Neo-Albanian representatives tie patriotism to democracy and liberalism. They also tie it to the emotional elements that bring cohesion among the people within a nation, as well as with in the state. Their view is distinguished from the

---

124V. Nirvana, Magazine "Illyria", 02. 11. 1935, p.5.

125Ibid.

126B. Merxhani, Man and Nation, (Dialogue with dead Man), Magazine "Albanian Endeavor", No. 14-15, Tiranë, February-March 1938, pp. 71-76.

western nationalist view that is generally characterized by the connection of the nation to religion.

Among the western concepts of nation, wide echo is given to the French political concept of nation and to the German concept of the cultural, ethnic nation. The French concept ∀ supported by Montesquieu, Voltaire, and so on- speaks about the spirit of the laws, about the gradual triumph of reason over prejudices. Prejudices regarding the superiority of France and the time of *"The Century of the Lights"* demonstrate the tendency of French rationalism to be blended within the national boundaries and to put the whole world under its yoke.

In opposition to this spirit of the France invasive of Napoleonic era, we have the emergence of *"Volksgeist,"* the German national genius, presented primarily in Herder's work, *"Another Philosophy of History,"* written in 1774. Herder wishes to give back to each nation the pride of its unrepeatable being. According to Herder, we must follow our own way... Let the people speak well or badly about our nation, our literature, our language: these are ours, our own self, and this is all there is to it.[127] It would take the utter defeat at Jena and the Napoleonic invasion for Volksgeist (national spirit) to start really its flight. Germany, divided into many principalities, finds again the sense of its unity in front of the conquering France. The elevation of the collective identity counterbalances the military defeat and the shameful subjugation that would have to be paid because of that defeat. Despite the humiliation that it has to suffer, the nation is to be indemnified through the discovery of the miracle of its own culture.

These concepts appeared strong at the time when Albanians were trying to achieve national unity. This was conditioned by Albania's reality where three major religions co-existed, which is why they connect the strengthening of the national state with the political, cultural, and economic development, as well as with the demonstration and the preservation of the specific values of each nation.[128] According to H. Ferraj, the characteristics of the

---

127Herder, quoted by Isaiah Berlin, Vico and Herder, Chatto and Windus, London, 1976, p.82.

128Magazine "Illyria", 24. 08. 1935, p.5.

Albanian national consciousness are the Messianic, protective, realistic, pragmatist, religiously tolerant, modernizing, and non-xenophobic-isolationist features, [129]more for a nation devoted to protect themselves as Albanians in the midst of explosive Balkans barrel.

At any rate, the suggestion is that the strengthening of the nation is central, while cosmopolitanism is valuable for those nations and societies that are more civilized than Albania.[130] In this framework, tradition appears as a component that influences the strengthening of national consciousness and national ideals.[131] Neo-Albanianism's tendency is to see cosmopolitanism in a discreet way and, thus, B. Merxhani puts in the mouth of a monk the words that view and evaluate it skeptically.

Cultural Solidarity, Not Religious Solidarity

The treatment of this issue by Neo-Albanian proponents is not very wide. They tend, primarily, toward a rational study of the religious views and religion in general. In this aspect, their evaluation tends to rely on O. Comte's concept of society, which in its stage of development has known a phase that was characterized by the rule of faith. This is justified on the general level of societal development, as well as on the mental level of society. In general, the representatives of Neo-Albanianism justify this phase by expounding upon the nature of religion and its effects upon humans. In accordance with the representatives of this thinking, religion reveals its values in the unification and disciplining of the masses through religious dogmas and

---

129H. Feraj, "The formal Aspects of political Opinion in Albania after World War II until 1990, (PhD diss, University of Tirana1997), p.61.

130B. Merxhani, Man and nation(Dialogue with dead Man), Magazine "Albanian Endeavor", No. 14-15, Tirana, February-March 1938, pp. 71-76.

131V. Nirvana, The intellectual Year 1936, Magazine "Albanian Endeavor", No. 4-5-6, Tiranë, March 1937, p. 204.

morality, as well as through the increase of cooperative energy between groups and individuals. This is achieved through the mystical element, which has had great organizational power among primitive masses whose thinking was not logical.[132]

The main proponents of Neo-Albanianism bring to the fore the pragmatic element of the role of religion. They do not occupy themselves directly with the issue of understanding religious dogmas, nor with the issues of the source of religious dogmas and their relationship to experience. Religions serve the existence of the relationship between humans, as well as the unification and disciplining of humans, thus religion is viewed as entirely justifiable, not only for the period when religious beliefs were predominant in defining their existence and place in society. Since, they deem the religions mission as reasonable, the Neo-Albanian stance toward religion and religions in Albania is a positive one. For example, they praised a number of conferences held by Pater Anton Harapi in Korça, calling them conferences with spiritual values,[133] which reveal the basis of Christianity.

In general, even if they see their plan of action as different from that of religion, Neo-Albanians accept similar goals and do not negate the role and utility of religion, and they positively value the practical aspect of its action. In special cases, they take a stance against rules or dogmas that very obviously manifest their conservative character. They have polemicized against the "Light Star" magazine on this issue, presenting a different notion of truth and arguing for a more progressive stance on this issue. According to them, every educated person may put the religious dogmas into doubt and, then, may even doubt God's existence as a reality outside of us, as well as the possibility of knowing God rationally or intuitively.[134]

132Newspaper "Demokratia", 09. 03. 1929, p. 3.

133V. Nirvana, Intellectual year 1936, Magazine "Albanian Endeavor", No. 4-5-6, Tiranë, March 1937, p. 204.

134Editorial Article, Magazine "Albanian Endeavor", No. 4-5-6, March 1937, p. 207.

Is God a given in the human experience?

Are all religious rules right?

Generally, in this aspect, Neo-Albanians oppose the Muslim religion concerning such rules as the keeping of veil by women and the Christian religion concerning such dogmas that define a common origin for men as creatures of God, thus damaging the basis of scientific studies on the national issues. Mainly for this reason, they think, there is a more convincing explanation for this issue than the one given by Christian theologians. Neo-Albanianism adheres mainly to O. Comte's opinion that religious solidarity has been replaced by cultural solidarity.[135] Thus, being a redundant explanation, it is no longer acceptable. Nonetheless, religion still retains special worth for the achievement of the aims of strengthening the nation and the relations among the people within it.

The state and its role in the development of pluralistic institutions

Neo-Albanians too, relying on the tradition of examining political sociology, devote special attention to the main empirical issue that deals with the description, analysis and explanation of that special, particular structure called "state".

Referring to B. Merxhani on his understanding of the state, we can find a definition closely related to the historical tradition on the state, based on the views of J. E. Renan and Zeitgeist, which is related to the time when the French and German nations were formed, alongside the complexes of their imagination, namely, the unification of state and nation, otherwise known by the term of "nation-state." It is written in Formulas of New-Albanianism: "Sociology, as a science, gives us a very special and independent 'definition' of the State. According to this 'definition,' the State constitutes the summation of the moral, scientific, artistic, religious, and juridical personality of a human crowd. ... A

135Magazine "Illyria", 26. 11. 1935, p. 5.

nation is nothing but a sentiment, idea, spiritual harmony, and 'social understanding' (B. Merxhani, 2003: 26-27, 30). We may combine it here with the definition by E. Renan of the "community of the will", as he calls the nation. To him, a nation is "a big solider community, knitted together by the feeling of sacrifices and the sacrifices made in the past, which it is also willing to make even in the future[...] the being of a nation is [...] a daily plebiscite." E. Renan also defines a nation's subjectivist component: "A nation is a spirit, a mental principle" (U. Altermatt 2002: 29). This presentation refers to an old notion that sees the presence of political institutions in almost all social relationships, so much so that it arrives at such views that equate (in the Neo-Albanian's case) the nation with the state.

In B. Merxhani we also find another treatment that seems to define the relations of the individual and the state, as follows: The will of the State is the will of Man concerning his own fate, which flows directly from the Generations' continuity. The social entirety, as a conscious circuit of the same activity, cannot be understood without a historical basis, which recognizes as national only that which is true... The state, apprehended as concrete cognition, is the function of the social brain of a specific quality of people. ...The future of the present State, in opposition to that of the primitive State, depends solely on a systematic and constant political and educational action on the part of the Citizen Man (B. Merxhani, 2003, p. 229).

If we analyse Merxhani's presentation, we see that social control as a function of the state is seen by him as connected with a concept such as "the social brain," "the political and continuous action," which means that there are distinctions in the way authority and power were exercised in the primitive state, but also in the way they were exercised later on. A political system, in our opinion, is any stable model of human relationships that contains power, order, or authority on an accepted and visible scale. This also accepts that there are distinctions in the way power is used by social groups, because this is, in one form or another, a potential characteristic of almost every society. Merxhani lays out the distinctions by inserting as a "solution" the specific people, who save society from undefined ability and the savage state.

We are dealing with the need to define state on the basis of evaluating the social definitions of institutions, which means that we must refer to the definition of state as the sole legitimate centre of authority and, alongside with this definition, comes and emerges the concept of the nation-state in modern societies. From what was said above, we can see that Merxhani himself does not distinguish the state from the nation, even though the history of the development of the Albanian nation differs from the classical model of the nation-state. Bearing these differences in mind, Merxhani in particular, but also other representatives of Neo-Albanianism has referred to the mixed model, which entails a consideration of the western model, as well as the model that came from the modern Turkey of M. K. Ataturk.

Indicators of a civilized—modern state

According to Merxhani, the indicator of a modern state is the ability to effectuate reforms. In Merxhani's opinion, this is related to the most innate qualities of the world's being. In one of the initiatory essays to introduce Neo-Albanianism to Albanians, Merxhani writes: Nature incessantly creates new forms. The forms it exhibits today have never existed before. And the forms it possessed at one time exist no more today. Nature incessantly creates new forms. – Here, then, the inviolable Law, ever strong, ever powerful; the Law of life, the Law of the human being; for the people, as much as for the nations, but, first of all, for the nations. Nations want to live, nations want to ever hold high the name of their history, to preserve the ground of their civilization and to develop it; these nations, in almost every period of their life, are swept by a huge reformatory wave (B. Merxhani, 2003: 18).

In Albania too we find endeavours on the part of the state to effectuate reforms. But the greatest need in the reformation of Albanian society, according to Merxhani, is the need for an intellectual foundation. Bearing in mind this deficiency in Albanian life, Merxhani writes: Every reformatory movement with a national and sociological content, in order to be serious, positive, efficient and fruitful, must have a general intellectual foundation. ... This is the law of the true activity of all the nations in the world (B. Merxhani, 2003: 19).

Moreover, Merxhani's arguments are not related only to the creation of a system that would include all those important social notions, but it is also important to make way for a miracle, as he calls the work of Gustav Le Bon, "Psychology of the crowds". Evaluating the work of the French psychologist, Merxhani writes: Albanian life and the Albanian soul are, from a simple psychological and sociological perspective, a *terra incognita* (unknown land) even for us, the children of this nation. This country has been suffering, for centuries, not only from a lack of unity and a conscientious national life (as some suppose), but it is also suffering, and deeply so, from a psychological anomaly. Albania, within the circle of European civilization, is a country that may be defined as a popular hospital of psychological diseases (B. Merxhani, 2003: 19).

Consequently, writes Merxhani, there is a need to create mental life. And, for Albania, mental life does not mean creating typographical spectacles, or the construction of entertainment centres, but rather, principles, steps, a courage for continual, serious research in order to analyse and explain the historical and sociological delays in national life... The work of the reforms, the preparatory work that aims at discovering the psychological and sociological laws of our national life, as basis for every reformatory endeavour on our part, this colossal work must be entrusted only to a monarchical youth (B. Merxhani, 2003, p.20).

B. Merxhani expresses his views with lucidity, yet they are not able to provide any adequate ways. Rather, they are marked more by signs of pathos and enthusiasm, than by the proper finding of the real means that would change Albanian society. This, in our opinion, is what Albanian life in the 1930s required and, despite the Neo-Albanians' faith in the figure of the king, we think that neither the king, nor the Neo-Albanians, were able to present clear programs for the reformation of society; rather, Neo-Albanians were in the habit of playing the classical role of the consumer and the commentator of what was happening, not having the courage or faith to make real that virtual reality, which they had envisioned in their minds, concerning the future of Albanian society,.

Rule in a society is related to the process of law composition. Certainly, many social activities exist alongside the activity of making and specifying laws. Law effectuation has to do with the social structure, its development, as well as with the rules on which this structure is built. The issue becomes even more complex if we turn to issues such as elections in Albania in the 1930s, participation in the voting process, characteristics of interaction between economic development and economic sustainability, or the political system; in other words, all these issues make it necessary for us to perform analyses that would properly consider what Neo-Albanians said, or could not say, as well as what they could not see or observe, because we cannot realistically deny that Albanian life in the 1930s did not offer huge opportunities for information, the necessary knowledge about the manner of development, and the real possibilities for Albanian society to break free from the whirlwind of conflictuallity, especially the social one.

In a society suffering from chronic illiteracy, which carried out elections through secondary electors, which had urgent need for a radical agrarian reform, which did not have a substantial development of capitalist relations, etc., which did not have any real political freedoms, which displayed a very backward and patriarchal mentality, we should deem as very courageous the concepts uttered by Neo-Albanians (and by their most vocal publicist, B. Merxhani). Therefore, we must admit that there is a relationship of dependency between the political and economic development of societies, which is made public by the exhibitions of values and the level of intellectual life which, in present-day Albania, seem still far from constituting hope-giving developments

IV. Social-Philosophical Views on Culture, Literature, and Arts

Culture–A Reflection of the Development of Society

Issues of cultures and arts also find reflection in the ideas of Neo-Albanianism. The proponents of this thinking valued the intellectual movement as highly important in the context of their actions toward the development of the country. According to B. Merxhani, only when we have a real mental preparation can we jump into the field of practice to apply our codified thoughts. Only then may we be certain that we will succeed.[136]

Their thoughts on culture, literature, and arts are expounded generally in the form of editorial comments or reviews on particular works, through which they, generally, achieve a sort of codification of their views on these issues. In the general sphere, their theory relies on the views of R. Descartes, E. Kant, O. Comte, and so forth. In the arts perspective, their views are more related to an evaluation of particular artistic and literary works than from the position of their philosophical background. Evaluating the quality of arts in Albania, they propose that the level of quality was generally low. They tie the cause of this backwardness to the effect of internal factors. Thus, their view is expressed in the evaluation that a certain art, or literature, does not backwardness from outside causes, but from inner causes. When old ideas are exhausted and the fountain of old feelings dries out, in order to form other, much more lively, ideas or feelings, people work on what is left, in a spiritual vacuum.[137] Furthermore, V. Koça opines that we live in a time when our

---

136Magazine "Albanian Endeavor", No. 11-12, Tirana, September 1937, pp. 207-208.

137V. Nirvana, The intellectual Year 1936, Magazine "Albanian Endeavor", No. 4-5-6, Tirana, March 1937, p. 204.

mental sterility is most obviously reflected by the poverty of literary production.[138]

For this reason, they deal a little less with the affirmation of artistic values, but, at any rate, value the arts on the basis of the importance of the duties they have set before themselves. According to them, it is necessary, first, to develop the culture and the intellectual achievements of Albanians and these, in the turn, will express themselves in a qualitative and cultivated literature and art, where artistic culminations and geniuses will not be exclude.

Another aspect in the thinking of the most distinguished proponents of Neo-Albanianism is related to the issue of the development of culture in general. Beginning with O. Comte's view and, later, opposing it, B. Merxhani would say, among other things: "...humankind does not consist of a single human society, which walks on a correct and unilateral development. There is no single human society as such... Mankind walks in diverse directions; in fact, with aims and tools that are not very related and that do not have many affinities with one another."[139]

Even though not entirely developed, this notion opposes evolutionist theories on linear social and cultural development. In fact, it seems that this notion is contrary to the Europe-centric concept of culture and, also, opposes those views that eradicate social and cultural *"superiorities."* Regarding the way of unifying and organizing the thoughts of the most distinguished proponents of Neo-Albanianism on this issue, scholar G. Bobi, in evaluating B. Merxhani's position, G. Bobi says: It is interesting to emphasize...we mean, the thesis that opposes the concept of culture as culture *par excellence* seems interesting, especially when posed by an author of the 1930s, who, in his writings, is an ardent adherent of 'Occidentalism' and of the concept on social

---

138Magazine "Albanian Endeavor", No. 11-12, Tirana, September 1937, p. 202.

139B. Merxhani, Comte and contemporary Sociology, Magazine "Albanian Endeavor", No. 16, Tiranë, April 1938, pp. 185-187.

and cultural development....[140] Naturally, this issue has other dimensions too.

The Aesthetic Perceptions of Art and the Concept of Art

Starting from the classical presentation of this issue, Neo-Albanianism proponents see the philosophical basis of art as connected to the issue of the nature of the perception of information, the contemplative experience in art. This is also expressed as a definition of the status of arts and the artistic work. The debate has always remained, and continues to remain, open to the issue of defining the arts and the qualities of the activity that are incarnated in the artistic work.

Which are those qualities that turn a human creation into a work of art and the human subject, which creates it, into an artist?

In this issue, the criterion of being comes to life, which must not be confused with the criterion of evaluation. Concerning the arts, the representatives of this tendency have in mind a number of definitions: the earliest definition consist of viewing as an imitation; another defines art as expression and means of communication; and yet another casts doubt on the first two, insisting that there cannot be a definition of art, because art and the artistic work are concepts that are continually changing and expanding. In addition, some tie art to that which is beautiful, thus further complicating the answer by it requiring a definition of that which is beautiful.

In trying to formulate a definition of that which is beautiful, some aesthetes connect it to a mystical, inexplicable beginning. Neo-Albanianism views find their place within this concept.

Let us shortly analyze some of these reflections on arts and the artistic work.

Firstly, there is the issue of treating art in the light of scientific arguments. From the cognitive point of view, we say that man is

---

140G. Bobi, Cultural Paradox, Rilindja, Prishtina, 1986, pp. 143-144.

characterized by the desire to know objects, life, and being. This happens because being in itself represents interest to the, i.e., for the subject of cognition without research intention, while for the cognitive subject as a simple individual, only the objects of research are important. As a consequence, according to this, the result, the end of any objective cognition of objects, things, as well as any cognition regarding an artistic work, an expression of the essence of life and being and can be reduced to an answer to the question: "What is life?" According to the main Neo-Albanian proponents, this question is answered in its specific, fully justified, way by every real and accomplished work of art.

Congratulating the publication of the poetic volume, "*Star of the heart*" by L. Poradeci, B. Merxhani writes: … [L. Poradeci's] poetic structure is built on the matter that he gathered all over the place among the dark ruins of our soul… The main importance of his poetic work is not in his accomplished lyricism, nor in his deep philosophical thoughts. Lasgush is the rustic poet…, who displays the truth of the rustic world.[141]

Secondly, a characteristic of the arts is that they all speak only in the genuine and infantile language of the intuition, not in the abstract and serious language of thought. Their answer is a passing image, not a general, stable knowledge. Thus, every work of art, every tableau, every statue, every poem, every theatrical stage, answers these questions only through intuition.

Thirdly, of all the arts, music answers more properly the question, "What is life?" because, with its common understandable language, it cannot be translated into the language of reason, expressing the most intimate essence of totality of life and being. In fact, within this orientation, M. Kuteli opines that L. Poradeci's poetry has a musical nature. He writes: Many of the older readers of Lasgush have long noticed that his work has a special sounding magic, a magic of its own, which is musical – as the others say. The musicality and plasticity of this work is the mirror of the inner assault, the spiritual assault of the poet, expressed through the word, which

141B. Merxhani, On the occasion of presenting the news of publication of the book "The star of the heart" of L.Poradeci, Magazine "Albanian Endeavor", No. 17, Tirana, May 1938, pp. 307, 308.

are woven one by one, and verse by verse, harmonized with the content and with the meaning of the work.[142]

Fourthly, all arts answer this question, but their answer is temporary, not complete or definitive. This is due to the fact a work of art only gives a fragment, a paradigm, instead of the rule or the whole, which may be given only through the generalization of concepts∀a matter belonging to the sciences.

Fifthly, a stable and permanently acceptable answer needs a deeper and *in abstracto* thought, which belongs to the realm of philosophy. The roots of philosophy and the beautiful arts are the same, but they differ in terms of abilities, directions and every other secondary thing. According to this reasoning, every artistic work has its own philosophical basis. The endeavor of Neo-Albanianism also aims, for example, at the discovery of the world of poetic inspirations of our poet" (of L. Poradeci – I. N.), in other words, the collection of the principles agreed to by him. This investigation is needed because Lasgushi's poetry is closely connected to his mental and spiritual formation.[143]

Sixthly, every work of art tries, in the real sense of the word, to show life and objects just as they truly are, but that may not be understood immediately by everybody, because of the fog of objective chance events. Among the arts, the works of the author of figurative arts and poetry pry open a treasure of deep knowledge, exactly because the knowledge of the nature of objects speaks through them. In this, works of art can only interpret expressions through clarification and the purest repetition.

In order to extract knowledge from works of arts of such a nature, one should understand the symbolics of their means, but this is determined by the level of education and the ability of each individual. In front of a tableau, everybody should stand as in front of a prince, expecting what to say to him and how; and

142M. Kuteli, Poetics of Lasgush Poradeci, Magazine "Albanian Endeavor", No. 17, Tirana, May 1938, p. 252.

143B. Merxhani, Explanatory note at the End of the Article of M. Kuteli "Poetics of Lasgush Poradeci", Magazine "Albanian Endeavor", Tirana, No. 17, May 1938, p. 253.

he himself should not address the prince first, because then he would be only hearing himself.

In order to clarify this thought, it should be added that this is not the same as art for art is sake, a view which found echo and was discussed in the press during the 1930s, as researcher and sociologist G. Bobi says.[144] At this time, there existed a polemic between a group of intellectuals, who advocated the view of art for art is sake- expressed especially in the writing of K. Maloki- and the views of the most distinguished proponents of Neo-Albanianism, who advocated the view of art in relation to life. In his article, "Language," published in the "Demokratia" newspaper on May 13, 1933, B. Merxhani wrote: Popular Poetry and European Poetry – here are two different Art Museums, within which our national literature may be formed and developed and prepared for a period of flourishing, a period which will not only solve the present turbulent issue of language, but in due time, it will notify us about the dawning of a new life and a new destiny.[145]

Seventhly, besides his direct contact with the work of art, the subject who establishes the contact with the work of art should also have the medium, the means of fantasy, which bring the work of art to life. This is a condition of the aesthetic effect and, for this reason; it constitutes a fundamental law of the beautiful arts. This also means that the senses are not given everything, and that the senses cannot catch everything. Fantasy is always left with something to do; in fact, the final step belongs to it.[146]

Eighthly, the good in art is spiritual and, thus, not all of it is perceived the senses. Sculpture and picture, especially, tend to activate fantasy, while poetry only addresses itself to fantasy, which it engages by means of simple words. B. Merxhani writes, expressing this theoretical vision, that L. Poradeci is "the Albanian poet who holds alive, within him, the spirit of an artist,

---

144G. Bobi, Cultural Paradox, Rilindja, Prishtina, 1986, p. 181.

145B. Merxhani, Language, Newspaper "Demokratia", 13. 05. 1933, p.5.

146B. Merxhani, Who is Descartes?, Magazine "Albanian Endeavor", No. 9-10, Tirana, Agust 1937, p.170.

who desires to summarize the aesthetic spirits that fly as in flight in the dry wind of this country. Lasgush is one of those who began his journey without looking anymore toward the desolate fields of our regions.[147]

Ninthly, art has, in its origins, the intuition, which is expressed through ideas. Artistic ideas are essentially intuitive and, as a result, inexhaustible in their approximate undefinable. Knowledge about them can be achieved only through the path of intuition, which is that of art. He who is involved and filled by an idea is excused if he chooses art as the means of representing and expressing his ideas.[148] For example, in the evaluation of a work of the plastic arts, or in the reading of a poem, or in the listening to a piece of music all of which try to describe something definite, we see the hidden appearance and, finally, the full appearance–through all the rich means of art–of the clear, limited, cold, and simple concept, which was the nucleus of the whole work, like the Poradeci's poetry. Only then is the whole creation solely supported by the clear thought in regard to it and, hence, expressed in its presentation. We are fully satisfied by the impressions of a work of art only when it leaves something which, despite all our meditation on it, does not help to clarify a concept.

Lastly, necessity is the mother of the useful arts, while the mother of the beautiful art is excess. The former has to do with the intellect, while the latter with genius, which is itself a kind of excess, viz., an excess of the power of cognition on the measure required to serve the will and the desire.[149] These views are expressed in some writings of Neo-Albanian thought, such as in the writings of B. Merxhani, M. Kuteli, and S. Luarasi.

147B. Merxhani, On the occasion of presenting the news of publication of the book "The star of the heart" of L.Poradeci, Magazine "Albanian Endeavor", No. 17, Tirana, May 1938, pp. 307, 308.

148Ibid., p. 308.

149A. Shopenhauer, The World as Will and Representation, Phoenix 1995, pp.52-58.

The Transcendent Spark Descends from the Heights

In the 1930s, the poet L. Poradeci published two volumes of poetry: "Dance of the Stars" (1933) and "Star of the Heart" (1937). One Neo-Albanian proponent, M. Kuteli, in the pages of the "Albanian Endeavor" magazine, throws light on the features of L. Poradeci's artistic creations; these features, in our opinion, reflect the aesthetic views of Neo-Albanianism. This idea is also affirmed by researcher G. Bobi in his monograph entitled "Cultural paradox."[150] The endeavor to evaluate L. Poradeci's creations includes the analysis of principles, spiritual elements, the philosophy embodied in his works, its contents and his mental and spiritual formation. According to B. Merxhani, the analysis of L. Poradeci's inspiration demonstrates transcendental characteritics, which means that is a state of being beyond the scope and understanding of our experience. When L. Poradeci speaks about a transcendental sparkle, we may see this as a rational principle that organizes our experience, despite the fact that it is insufficient to achieve cognition.

A star descends from heights above,

A shining flash of light -

As a flame and a shadow,

It lightens up my heart.

I can see it, with my tired soul,

As it very slowly drips,

It opens, in the folded word,

The corner of a pleat.[151]

Further, we may concentrate on some of the elements of fantasy that appear in L. Poradeci's poetry. First of all, there are a

---

150G. Bobi, Cultural Paradox, Rilindja, Prishtina 1946, p. 143.

151M. Kuteli, Poetics of L.Poradeci, Magazine "Albanian Endeavor", Tirana, No. 17, May 1938, pp. 243-244.

number of elements that are related to the poet's early experience, especially the fantastical interpretation of his childhood events or experiences. Relying on the richness of the Albanian language, he accomplishes a universe of verses where the elements gain a multifaceted nature; they are direct components of the real, physical, world, and are also imaginary components, passing through a series of transformations, gaining extra-human dimensions and qualities, or rising up to the level of the most abstract symbol. The poet views the falling of dusk as a veil spreading out like a shadow; the dark lake in the evening on the mountain reminds him of the fluid and divine spirit shut within his chest; the stars of the sky, fading in the morning, are like darkened eyes; the pelican is the morning's herald; the stork walks like a bridegroom with a crown and crane; alongside him, a world appears, like a newly wedded bride which, according to M. Kuteli, is also similar to Buddhist spiritualistic-meditative scenes.[152] B. Merxhani quotes L. Poradeci's thought, who said that on the one hand, we must awaken our people's aesthetic motives and, on the other, make them understand the masterpieces of European literature. According to B. Merxhani, these qualities, exhibited in L. Poradeci's aesthetic thinking and artistic work, make him the only artist of the generation of the '30s who has the height hand depth of a pure human-aesthetic.[153]

The Beautiful Aspect Exhibited in L. Poradeci's Poetry

According to M. Kuteli, it is expressed in a harmonization of form and content. This exact interweaving has as its primary element the fact that L. Poradeci's poetry expresses the troubles of the soul, the joy and bitterness, and the most refined emotions of the man-poet.[154]

152M. Kuteli, Poetics of L.Poradeci, Magazine "Albanian Endeavor", Tirana, No. 17, May 1938, pp. 243-244.

153B. Merxhani, "Language", Newspaper "Demokratia", 13. 05. 1933, p. 5.

154M. Kuteli, Poetics of L.Poradeci, Magazine "Albanian Endeavor", Tirana, No. 17, May 1938, pp. 243-244.

Generally, Neo-Albanian thinkers describe L. Poradeci as an expressive poet. He dimensions a spectrum of extreme limits or in a macro-cosmic space, like a rainbow spread out among the stars and the knowledge of the universe, or this happens more often in the condensed density of a teardrop. This demonstrates a tendency conditioned by the poet's desire, which is ubiquitous in order to transport the expressiveness of the poetic verbality beyond the boundaries of the impossible.

According to M. Kuteli, L. Poradeci's poetry originates from the popular substratum, which continued to feed his poetry. Reading L. Poradeci's poetry through time we think that, despite the distinguished diversity of the interpretation of the messages it has provoked, at one point it has shown the tendency to converge; we have to deal with a creativity that, beyond the moment, aims at eternity and, beyond the local, aims at the universal (it is similar to G. W. F. Hegel's scheme about the rapports between the particulars and the universals). In our opinion, the colors of L. Poradeci's poetry in the two volumes published during the 1930s are very near the conceptions and structures of oral popular poetry. In fact, L. Poradeci deems the creation of the rhymed poetry as the truest of all poetry, and he cites Bualo saying, "*Rhyme is a slave and it must only obey,*" that is, he values the feature that characterizes, first of all, the Albanian popular poetry.[155] In L. Poradeci, as a rule, the symbolics of the spectrum of colors is not encountered in the elementary functions; I. Kadare has said that Lasgush always told him, in their conversations, about his first fiancé, a painter, who was blonde and, then, became dark-complexioned when they separated.[156] His vision for colors, in our opinion, is completely conceptual and abstract, but with certain emotional connections.

According to M. Kuteli, the perceptibility of this mixture of colors and lexicon has an expressiveness that springs from within

155P. Kolevica, Lasgushi told me, "8 Nëntori", Tirana 1992, p. 101.

156I. Kadare, Migjeni—The interrupted Hurricane, "Naim Frashëri", Tirana 1991, p. 18.

and, if you remain within the limit of a simple perception, then you may arrive at the conclusion that we are in the area of the poetic constructions that lack logic, for example, in the verses:

Ah! You cannot stop my terrible pain

From becoming fire and light – even a white light![157]

Similar to this are also other constructions of a paradoxical kind, such as, *the clean fez, the blackened fez.* According to formal logic, the fez cannot be at the same time clean and blackened. He also achieves expressiveness through another verse, *the lip that smiles and sighs*; this is a meditative feature of L. Poradeci's poetry. In such synthetic constructions, the expressive function of color is intertwined with function, which becomes more perceptible in the following verses:

Her white skin, her red skin,

Her under-chin like a lily, her lips like a flower bud.

Furthermore, in L. Poradeci's poetry, elements of the lyrical hero's spirit are also expounded. The wide gamut of the elements that characterizes his verses concentrates on the poet's spirit as their object. They are part of an almost cosmic imagination, realized through strong, and apparently impressive, feelings, such as in the following verses:

Black dust covers your solitary eyes,

Your solitary eyes kindle stars on the sea waves,...

When I saw them, oh! In a night of wormwood, the distant moon was cast in gold.

When I saw them in a night of wormwood, my mourning turned into cast gold.[158]

Dwelling on L. Poradeci's poetry, B. Merxhani underlines the characteristic of transcendental conception in its beginning, as

---

157M. Kuteli, Poetics of L.Poradeci, Magazine "Albanian Endeavor", Tirana, No. 17, May 1938, pp. 243-244.

158M. Kuteli, Poetics of L.Poradeci, Magazine "Albanian Endeavor", Tirana, No. 17, May 1938, pp. 243-244.

well as in its general concept. Among other things, B. Merxhani writes: ... when we say that Lasgushi's poetic inspiration descends from the transcendental world *like a sparkle from the heights*, we must understand that the world of our poet's poetic inspirations consists of a group of principles that are accepted *a priori*, of unshakeable, true, and simple spiritual powers that pervade and completely dominate the poet's mental being.[159]

In our opinion, B. Merxhani views the *a priori* conception of the world of perceptions as a quality of L. Poradeci's poetry, which gives it its main features. This is an intertwining of this view with that of E. Kant, not only when he mentions the *sinnliche Erfahrung*,[+] but also with that of E. Kant's works, *Kritik der reinen Vernunft*.[++]

Moreover, B. Merxhani notes: *Transcendentalism* is a kind of view that relies only on the conscious notions and contents without asking whether these have some kind of objective support or not. Transcendental ideas become empirical images only when they are connected to objective things understood by means of some mental experience.[160]

In fact, B. Merxhani and M. Kuteli do not consider the analysis of Lasgush Poradeci's poetry as something completed. It has clear elements of the concepts of the world and art similar to the views of the main proponents of Neo-Albanianism. At the same time, it needs deeper analyses of a philosophical character, which should take into consideration the poet's mental and spiritual background, and it should also be a creativity that is completed by the poet's ongoing creativity.[161] This vacuum is somewhat

---

159B. Merxhani, On the occasion of presenting the news of publication of the book "The star of the heart" of L.Poradeci, Magazine "Albanian Endeavor", No. 17, Tirana, May 1938, pp.307, 308.

+[+] sinnliche Erfahrung(gjerm)-sensous experience.

++[++] Kritk der reinen Vernunft(gjerm)-Critique of Pure Reasons.

160B. Merxhani, Magazine "Albanian Endeavor", No. 17, Tirana, May 1938, p. 253.

161B. Merxhani, Magazine "Albanian Endeavor", No. 17, Tirana, May 1938, f. 253.

filled in our days, even though, neither we, nor the others who have dealt with the deep artistic and philosophical analysis of L. Poradeci, have pretended that the area of his study has been exhausted.

R. Elsie underline this view in his History of Albanian literature when write: Poradeci's subjects, his structures and language were very much attuned to southern Albanian oral literature, in particular to Tosk folk verse from which he drew a good deal of his inspiration. Mitrush Kuteli, who edited his *Star of the Heart* called him "the only Albanian poet to think, speak and write only in Albanian." Lasgush Poradeci is at the same time an artist of truly European stature. He combined the verbal sensuousness of Charles Baudelaire, the aesthetic philosophy of form and the discerning elegance of Stefan George, the humanity and philosophy of Naim Frashëri, and the cosmic immortality of his master, Mihai Eminescu. Scholar Eqrem Çabej said of him that he was the "poet whom Albania would one day bequeath to the world," and although Poradeci's verse does not lend itself particularly to translation, time may prove [E.] Çabej right (Elsie, R., 2006: 142).

Roy Fuller, known for his syllabic verses in his work "Owls and Artificers", has written that poetry is music in words and that music is poetry in sounds. Both are good sauces, but those who cooked their soup with these two sauces, have died in poverty (according to I. Luzaj: 1999, p. 53). In order to understand poets, their Ego in poetry should be understood. In order to understand the poet's Ego, the human being must be mentally prepared to take a walk and to strongly leave the passions of his own time, be they of a religious, political, social, racial, or national nature. Maybe this was why the great poet, Poradeci, used to say that they would build his monument only after fifty years.

Afterword

There is no question that Neo-Albanianism takes a conspicuous position in the intellectual challenge of the '30s in the 20th century. This part of the social, philosophical, aesthetic, artistic (etc.) thought was developed through polemics with the viewpoints of other currents, especially that of the "illustrious dictatorship", the legalists, the communistic viewpoints, and so forth.

As a trend, Neo-Albanianism demonstrates, *first of all*, elements of a national nature that can be evaluated, and constitutes, in my opinion, the most refined and most complete national viewpoint. Focusing on this aspect, we may say that Neo-Albanianism may be defined as *new nationalism,* or *the nationalism of the 1930s*. This conclusion may be attained based on the relations that Neo-Albanianism creates with the past of the Albanian people– a past that is historical, economic, political, cultural, and intellectual.

According to the views of the main representatives of this trend, the periods when Albanian patriotism created its fundamental elements were the age of Skanderbeg and that of the Albanian National Renaissance. While this nationalism was in its infancy during Skanderbeg's time, the National Renaissance period brought more complete components, as well as its completeness. This, in its turn, determined a reasonable and quite positive preface to Albania's future – the declaration of Independence on 28 November 1912 by Ismail Qemali. To support this idea, this trend's main representatives bring forward the argument of the existence of the national ideal during the National Renaissance.

According to the definitions provided by the main proponents of Neo-Albanianism, patriotism is related to the developments of the 1930s and the need for progress in the Albanian society of the period. According to them, these developments were related to the values achieved by Albanians throughout their history, but were also very closely related to the Albanian reality of their time. Consequently, the Neo-Albanian stance toward the Albanian state in the 1930s was a positive one. It can be called positive because, generally speaking, they accept the Albanian state in its political and monarchical form, with King Zog I as its head, and, at the same time, they present arguments for such a stance.

Furthermore, the instrumentalization of democracy was deemed a natural and most important process for the Albanian society, through which, by means of the election process (similar to the election model of western societies, but also with some Albanian specifics), it was hoped to achieve a natural progress in this area.

According to Neo-Albanians, an election model that was similar to that of western countries could be attained in big towns such as "Gjirokastra, Vlora, Korça, Durres, Shkoder, etc.," whereas, in less developed regions, the election system of secondary electors could still be used.

The views of the main proponents of Neo-Albanianism revolve around a philosophical conception that aims at synthesis the theory of cognition, metaphysics and ethics. Furthermore, its proponents view philosophy in every form of the intellectual activity also as a philosophy of science, history, religion, arts, and so on. Neo–Albanianism treats philosophy in its definition as a critical philosophy, as well as a speculative philosophy; it is also called a judgment of thought. This way, philosophy is separated and differentiated from the diverse kinds of thought into specific parts or aspects that precipitate in science, history, and so on. When philosophy is treated as metaphysics, it is better referred to as a critical investigation of the kinds of knowledge, as assertions and methods of thought that create a general view of the world (one might say, a worldview). For this reason, philosophy is viewed as a thought, view, and judgment of thought, and it is thus excluded and differentiated from the many others kinds of thinking. In such a way, their difference is achieved more fully and the position of philosophy is defined, in our view, as well as its ideas, methods and constitution of the object it tries to achieve

Issues of cultures and arts also find reflection in the ideas of Neo-Albanianism. The proponents of this thinking valued intellectual movement as highly important in the framework of their actions for the development of the country. According to B. Merxhani, only when we have a real mental preparation can we jump into the field of practice to apply our codified thoughts. Only then may we be certain that we will succeed.

Their thoughts on culture, literature, and arts are expounded generally in the form of editorial comments or reviews on particular works, through which they, generally, achieve a sort of codification of their views on this issue. If, in the general sphere, their theory relied on the views of R. Descartes, E. Kant, O. Comte, etc., from the arts perspective, we think that their views are more related to an evaluation of particular works from the position of their philosophical background. Evaluating the quality of arts in Albania, they thought that this level was generally low.

In the 1930s, the poet L. Poradeci published two volumes of poetry: "Dance of the Stars" (1933) and "Star of the Heart" (1937). One Neo-Albanian proponent, M. Kuteli, in the pages of the "Albanian Endeavor" magazine, often tries to throw light on the features of L. Poradeci's artistic creations; these features, in our opinion, reflect the aesthetic views of Neo-Albanianism.

Dwelling on L. Poradeci's poetry, B. Merxhani underlines that a characteristic of his poetry is transcendental conception in its beginning, as well as in its general concept. Among other things, B. Merxhani writes: "… when we say that Lasgushi's poetic inspiration descends from the transcendental world *like a sparkle from the heights*", etc…," we must understand that the world of our poet's poetic inspirations consists of a group of principles that are accepted *a priori*, of unshakeable, true, and simple spiritual powers that pervade and completely dominate the poet's mental being.

In the backdrop of the Albanian developments in the 1930's, Neo-Albanians chose the pluralism of viewpoints, which they publicized in the press of the day, especially in the Albanian Endeavour newspaper. According to Neo-Albanians, the formula Albania needed was *progress-order-rule* and, viewed from the perspective of conditions in Albania, this meant that progress could be advocated and achieved by any bourgeois-type regime. Neo-Albanians in general were of the opinion that the path of bourgeois development was already the principle of progress in the Albanian society and, despite its slowness; it was already walking on this path.

In a more generalizing characterization, Neo-Albanianism represents an entirety of viewpoints of a democratic nature, which tend toward the prioritized evaluation of the illuminating role of knowledge, science, and culture.

Mostly, Neo-Albanians thought that the way to bourgeois development was the principle to the progress of the Albanian society which enhances the slowness; really it is following this way.

Based on the suggestions offered by the ways followed by the advanced developed societies we could conclude that the societies, which have a stable economic development, have developed the values and the appropriate structures connected with industrialization, such as the efficiency, rationalism, re-investments and benefit, the development of the organizations of big businesses and so forth; all these create the basis for the increasing rate of the integration of social groups on the basis of pluralism as a political solution. Otherwise, the Albanian society of the 21-st century has not secured yet these stable economic developments, the values and structures connected with it and also because of the fragility are the democratic system and political pluralism, and in these conditions Neo-Albanianism preserves precious contemporary values.

Bibliography

Press

Bejleri Z. "Kredija agrare", Revista "Përpjekja Shqiptare", Nr. 11-12, shtator 1937.

Charpentier T. V. "Metafizika e Dekartit", Revista "Përpjekja Shqiptare", Nr. 9-10, gusht 1937.

De Man H. "Shkaqet e krizës evropiane", Revista "*Përpjekja Shqiptare*", Nr. 4-5-6, mars 1937.

Koça V. "Në udhën e nacionalizmës", Revista "*Përpjekja Shqiptare* ", Nr. 7, prill 1937.

Koça V. "Viti mendor 1936", Revista "*Përpjekja Shqiptare*", Nr. 4-5-6, mars 1937.

Koça V. Perkthim i veprës së Dekartit "Dicours de la methode", Revista "*Përpjekja Shqiptare*", Nr. 9-10, gusht 1937.

Kuteli M. "Poetika e L. Poradecit", Revista "*Përpjekja Shqiptare*", Nr. 17, maj 1938.

Merxhani B. "Ç'është psikanaliza", Revista "*Përpjekja Shqiptare*", Nr. 7, prill 1937.

Merxhani B. "Ç'është psikanaliza", Revista "*Përpjekja Shqiptare*", Nr. 4-5-6, mars 1937.

Merxhani B. "Ç'është sociologjia", Revista "*Përpjekja Shqiptare*", Nr. 8, maj 1937.

Merxhani B. "Ç'është sociologjia", Revista "*Përpjekja Shqiptare*", Nr. 7, prill 1937.

Merxhani B. "Dekarti dhe ne", Revista "*Përpjekja Shqiptare*", Nr. 9-10, gusht 1937.

Merxhani B. "Ideali", Gazeta "Demokratia", 09. 03. 1929.

Merxhani B. "Individualizmi", Revista "*Përpjekja Shqiptare*", Nr. 7, prill 1937.

Merxhani B. "Kombi", Gazeta "Demokratia", 23. 01. 1929.

Merxhani B. "Konti dhe sociologjia e sotme", Revista "*Përpjekja Shqiptare*", Nr. 16, prill 1938.

Merxhani B. "Kush është Dekarti", Revista "*Përpjekja Shqiptare*", Nr.. 9-10, gusht 1937.

Merxhani B. "Me rastin e botimit të "Yllit të zemrës" të L. Poradecit", Revista "*Përpjekja Shqiptare*", Nr. 17, maj 1938.

Merxhani B. "Nëpër fshatra", Revista "*Përpjekja Shqiptare* re", Nr. 8, maj 1937.

Merxhani B. "Nga kultura në politikë", Revista "Përpjekja Shqiptare", Nr. 11-12, shtator 1937.

Merxhani B. "Njeriu dhe kombi", Revista "Përpjekja Shqiptare", Nr. 14-15, shkurt-mars 1938.

Merxhani B. "Njeriu qyetar", Revista "Illyria", Nr. 1, 04. 03. 1934.

Merxhani B. "Njeriu qyetar", Revista "Illyria", Nr. 2, 11. 03. 1934.

Merxhani B. "Për filozofinë morale të Dekartit", Revista "Përpjekja Shqiptare", Nr. 9-10, gusht 1937.

Merxhani B. "Pesë mësime mbi psikanalizën", Revista "Përpjekja Shqiptare", Nr. 16, prill 1938.

Merxhani B. "Pesë mësime mbi psikanalizën", Revista "Përpjekja Shqiptare", Nr. 17, maj 1938.

Merxhani B. "Pesë mësime mbi psikanalizën", Revista "Përpjekja Shqiptare", Nr. 18-24, dhjetor 1938.

Merxhani B. "Politika dhe kultura", Revista "Përpjekja Shqiptare ", Nr. 2, 1936.

Merxhani B. "Pse nuk jam Marksist", Revista "Përpjekja Shqiptare", Nr. 4-5-6, mars 1937.

Merxhani B. "Shteti", Gazeta "Demokratia", 01.01. 1929.

Merxhani B. Paraqitje e librit të Dr. D. Zavalanit "Die landwirtschaftlichen Verhältnisse Albaniens", Revista "Përpjekja Shqiptare", Nr. 17, maj 1938.

Merxhani B. Recension për librin "Historia e doktrinave ekenomike", Revista "Përpjekja Shqiptare", Nr. 4-5-6, mars 1937.

Merxhani B. Shkrim vlerësues në rubrikën "Jeta dhe librat", me rastin e vdekjes së A. Adlerit, Revista "Përpjekja Shqiptare", Nr. 14-15, shkurt-mars 1938.

Meyer J. G. "Vlera filozofike dhe vlera njerëzore e kartezianizmit", Revista "Përpjekja Shqiptare", Nr. 9-10, gusht 1937.

Paparisto S. "Ç'është sugjestioni", Revista *"Përpjekja Shqiptare"*, Nr. 16, prill 1938.

Peshkëpia N. "Misteri i kohës", Revista *"Përpjekja Shqiptare"*, Nr. 11-12, shtator 1937.

Plumbi O. "Feminizma dhe shoqëria jonë", Revista *"Përpjekja Shqiptare"*, Nr. 16, prill 1938.

Shuteriqi Dh. "Edukata e Sociologji" nga E. Durkhejm, Revista *"Përpjekja Shqiptare"*, Nr. 17, maj 1938.

Shuteriqi Dh. "Edukata ësht një funksion social", përkthim nga vepra e E. Durkhejmit "Education et Sociologie", Revista *"Përpjekja Shqiptare"*, Nr. 4-5-6, mars 1937.

Skëndo L. "Për historinë e Shqipërisë", Revista *"Përpjekja Shqiptare"*, Nr. 4-5-6, mars 1937.

Toto I. "Organizimi i jetës kulturale", Revista "Illyria", Nr. 1, 04. 03. 1934.

Treska S. "Biologjia dhe edukata", Revista *"Përpjekja Shqiptare"*, Nr. 14-15, shkurt-mars 1938.

Treska S. "Biologjia dhe edukata", Revista *"Përpjekja Shqiptare"*, Nr. 13, janar 1938.

Treska S. "Fiziologjia dhe edukata", Revista *"Përpjekja Shqiptare"*, Nr. 18-24, dhjetor 1938.

Treska S. "Fusha e problemit edukativ", Revista *"Përpjekja Shqiptare"*, Nr. 11-12, shtator 1937.

Xhuvani A. "Personaliteti", Revista *"Përpjekja Shqiptare"*, Nr. 16, prill 1938.

Zavalani T. "Problemi demografik shqiptar, Lëvizja demografike në vitet 1931-1936, Revista *"Përpjekja Shqiptare"*, Nr. 14-15, shkurt-mars 1938.

Zavalani T. "Problemi demografik shqiptar", Revista *"Përpjekja Shqiptare"*, Nr. 17, maj 1938.

Zavalani T. "Problemi demografik shqiptar", Vërejtje të përgjithshme, Revista *"Përpjekja Shqiptare"*, Nr. 13, janar 1938.

Zavalani T. Koment i raportit të Lidhjes së Kombeve për ushqimin, Revista *"Përpjekja Shqiptare"*, Nr. 11-12, shtator 1937.

Studies and Books

Arendt, H. *Valter Benjamin* (1892-1940), Korbi, Tiranë 1999.

Benhabib, S. *Hannah Arendt-Die melancholische Denkerin der Moderne*, Rotbuch Verlag, Hamburg 1998.

Benjamin, V. *Illuminacione*, Korbi 1998.

Berkeley, G. *The Principles of Human Knowledge*, The Fontana Library, 3rd Impression, May 1967.

Comte, A. (Trad. J. H. Bridges), *System of Positive Polity*, New York: Harper and Row, 1877.

Cvajg, S. *Frojdi*, ShB "Fan Noli", Tirana 1992.

Dahrendorf, R. *Konflikti shoqëror modern*, Dituria, Tirana 1997.

Descartes, R. *Meditations on First Philosophy*, H. P. Com Inc 1979.

Dtv- Atlas zur Philosophie, 1991, Dt Gmbh&CokG München.

Dumont, L. *Ese mbi individualizmin*, Korbi, Tirana 1997.

Durkheim, E. *The Rules of Sociological Method*, The Free Press 1966.

Elsie, R. The History of Albanian literature. Scanderbeg books, Tirana 2006.

Ferraj, H. *Aspekte të mendimit politik zyrtar në Shqipëri mbas Luftës II Botërore deri më 1990*. Disertacion që ndodhet pranë Departamentit të Sociologji-Filozofisë të Fakultetit të Shkencave Sociale, Tirana 1996.

Ferri, L. *Homo Aestheticus-Shpikja e shijes në epokën e demokracisë*, Elena Gjika dhe Shtëpia e Librit dhe Komunikimit, Tirana 2002.

Finkielkraut, A. *Disfata e mendimit*, Marin Barleti, Tirana 1999.

Freud, S. *Character and Culture*, 1963 by M. P& Co Inc.

Freud, S. *Grouppsychology and the analysis of the Ego*, 1959 W. W. N. & C.

Freud, S. *Introductory Lectures on Psychoanalysis*, W. W. N&C 1966.

Freud, S. *Psikanaliza e artit dhe e letërsisë*, Dituria, Tirana 2000.

Gardner, H. *Frames of Mind, BasicBooks*, New York 1993.

Gardner, H. *So genial wie Einstein: Schlüssel zum kreativen Denken*, Stutgart: Klett-Cotta, 1996.

Ginsberg, M. *Essays in Sociology and Social Philosophy*, Penguin Books, 1968 USA.

Hanfling, O. *Estetika filozofike*, Camaj-Pipa 1999.

Hersh, Zh. *Habia filozofike*, Dituria, Tirana 1994.

Kadare, I. *Ardhja e Migjenit në letërsinë shqipe*, ShB "Naim Frshëri", Tirana 1991.

Kandinski, V. *Mbi shpirtëroren në art*, Botime Përpjekja, Tirana ! 998.

Kazantzakis, N. *Asketika*, Panteon, Tirana 1999.

Koça, V. *Në udhën e Shqiptarizmës*, Phoenix, Tirana 1999.

Koka, V. *Rrymat e mendimit politiko-shoqëror në Shqipëri në vitet 30-të të shekullit të 20-të*, Sh B "Kombinati Poligrafik, Shtypshkronja e Re", Tirana 1985.

Konica, F. *Vepra*, ShB "Naim Frashëri", Tirana 1993.

Kreitler H&Sh. *Psychology of the Arts*, D. U. P.D. N. C 1972.

Kroçe, B. *Estetika si shkencë e shprehjes dhe e gjuhësisë së përgjithshme*, Apollonia, Tirana 1998.

Labirinti Borges, Onufri 1999.

Larousse- *Fjalori i filozofisë*, ShBE, Tirana 1994.

Le Bon, G. *Psychologie des Foules*, Presses Universitaires De France 1963.

Merxhani, B. *Formula të Neo-Shqiptarizmës*, Apollonia, Tirana 1996.

Nietzsche, F. *Antikrishti*, ASD, Tirana 2000.

Nietzsche, F. *Kështu foli Zarathustra*, Phoenix, Tirana 1996.

Nietzsche, F. *Schopenhauer as Educator*, Regenery/Gateway, Inc. 1965.

Nikaj, I. *Përfaqësuesit kryesorë të Neoshqiptarizmës për traditën filozofike*, Buletini shkencor Nr.2, Universiteti "Fan S. Noli", Korça 1999.

Nikaj, I. *Pikëpamje të përfaqësuesve të neoshqiptarizmës për zbutjen e kundërshtive shoqërore*. Review Pajtimi 1/2002.

Nikaj, I. *Sociologjia*, Afërdita, Tirana 2001.

Pascal, B. *Pensees*, Garnier Freres 1961.

Poradeci, L. *Vepra*, ShB "Naim Frashëri", Tirana 1990.

Schopenhauer, A. *The Essential Shopenhauer*, Unwin Books, London 1962.

Shopenhauer, A. *Bota si vullnet e si paraqitje*, (kapituj të shkëputur) Phoenix, Tirana 1995.

Spencer, H. *The principles of Sociology*, Vol. 1, London, 3rd ed., New York: Harper and Row, 1985.

The Fontana Dictionary of Modern Thought, Edit. A. Bullock & O. Stallybrass, 5th Impressions, october 1982, W. C. Sand Co Ltd, Glasgow.

Voltaire, F. M. *Distionnaire Philosophique*, Edit. Garnier Freres 1961.

Xoxi, K. Branko Merxhani: *Formula të Neoshqiptarizmës 1996*.

Alphabetical Index
Alphabetical Index